COLLEGE STUDENT GOVERNMENT

COLLEGE

BY GORDON KLOPF

VISITING PROFESSOR OF EDUCATION
TEACHERS COLLEGE
COLUMBIA UNIVERSITY

STUDENT GOVERNMENT

*Foreword by Samuel B. Gould
former President, Antioch College
and Chancellor,
University of California,
Santa Barbara*

Harper & Brothers, New York

18418

CONTENTS

FOREWORD

Our zeal as educators and citizens concerned with the democratic processes of American society sometimes does strange things to our powers of perception. It would seem, for example, that believing as we do in the efficacy of such a process, we should quickly see the values in preparing students as early as possible for their inevitable and vital responsibilities as democratic citizens. We presumably should recognize that offering responsible functions to students would have the effect of hastening their maturation and their sensitivity to civic participation. Indeed, when one reads the literature of our profession, one finds it well seasoned with declarations of how important is the maturing process for youth and how necessary it is to give them real responsibility in their campus government.

A glance at actual practice in American higher education, however, reveals quite a different situation almost paradoxical in its significance. College and university administrations, in the midst of their declarations of eagerness to give youth a proper sphere of campus activity, all too frequently interpret this "proper sphere" as one far removed from the serious and vital campus decisions. Furthermore, they are all too prone to show in their own administrative actions a disregard for the democratic process that must shake the faith of students who observe or are subject to them. Nor are faculties themselves guiltless in this regard. We have all encountered the faculty member who can deliver panegyrics on academic freedom and democratic ideals, and then conduct himself in departmental affairs with every ruthless means he can find to protect his own mediocrity or to indulge his false notions of power. Such maneuverings do not pass unnoticed by the student body, and if our youth tend toward cynicism and apathy as a result, we have only ourselves to blame.

It is, of course, the better part of discretion to put the student leaders out to pasture in some remote corner of the institutional ranch where, with adequate fencing, they can graze peacefully and wax fat and docile. They will then always be properly deferent, will be grateful for any little attentions tendered them, and will never ask embarrassing or challenging questions. They will graduate with the same sheeplike acceptance of directions that they brought with them as freshmen. They will also make no contribution to their own growth or that of the campus except to advance the state of atrophy in themselves and their institution.

Colleges and universities with this approach can always be recognized: they talk loudly and long about their superiority, boast of the even and efficient tenor of the campus way, and carefully eliminate the mavericks. They champion the "well adjusted" and socially competent product whose major claim to recognition is that he has not been troublesome. And at commencements they piously raise and wave banners with magnificent slogans like "The Challenge of the Future" or "Youth Must Remake the World." Nor do these seem to them at all inconsistent with their practices.

The other side of the coin is equally distressing. This is when the line between faculty and students vanishes, when a kind of bogus camaraderie develops as a way of assuring the student that he is an equal, and when in this insistence upon equality the student is plunged into decision-making in areas where he is unprepared. Such heady wine poured out by the gobletful to those only lately weaned from lemonade causes weaklings to inflate their chests, to make loud noises on every possible issue, and to plunge recklessly into new and untried ventures. Soon every aspect of academic life is within their purview, and they brook no restraints, however gentle. Instead of the partnership of intellect so eagerly to be desired on a campus, a kind of juvenile dictatorship results, leaving the faculty either fearful or amused depending upon their own state of popularity.

Here, then, are two forms of adult delinquency in education, neither of which even remotely meets the basic problem of making youth aware as quickly as possible that it cannot nor should not ignore its close proximity to adulthood. In both instances a disservice to youth is being performed. On the one hand, the student is being treated like a pampered child by having everything done for him; on the other, he is being equally pampered by being encouraged through an excess of permissiveness to be irresponsible. The answer is careful selection of areas of student participation, with intelligent ground rules by which the student operates, and intelligent guidance of his progress.

Obviously the involvement of students in campus administration is an additional and sometimes annoying burden for the permanent faculty and staff. It is not easy to share certain areas of authority with students when the process may double the amount of time necessary to resolve the problems presented. Similarly, it is not easy to stand by patiently and allow a certain amount of trial and error to take place when earlier experiences has long since indicated the right path to follow. But the educational rewards are too great to be ignored; the added dimension of student experience is too valuable to be shunted aside without careful consideration. Most important of all, one cannot champion one of the most important ingredients of democracy such as creative leadership without offering students practical opportunities to develop such an attribute.

To follow such a policy of involvement, however, does not mean abdication of authority on the part of the administration. On the contrary, it sometimes means granite-like firmness, for the students will be eager to edge their way into territory that should be forbidden to them. And all such firmness should be founded upon the adherence to a single principle: *There can be no authority without responsibility; the consequences of error cannot be ignored.*

While there is nothing new about this principle, students frequently choose to ignore it and in doing so exhibit their immaturity. With some it is an honest error of judgment; with others it is deliberate evasion so as to open the door for irresponsible actions conveniently labeled "experimental." But a college administration insisting on maintaining the connection between authority and responsibility can give its students all sorts of vital and creative opportunities for leadership without endangering the structure of the institution or losing its own proper identity with authority. It can repeatedly drive home one of the most important laws by which mature people must live, namely that they evaluate their prospective actions in terms of the price they will have to pay for them.

Professor Klopf's book has as unusual amount of good advice to offer on the whole subject of college student government. It is virtually a manual with details of policies and procedures. But its every page directly or indirectly proclaims that until we begin offering the college students the opportunities and responsibilities of adulthood they will continue to be children. The truly vital lesson we all must learn is that of faith in the present generation of youth. We must realize that they are ready to be tested with adulthood's problems, and we must approach this testing process intelligently.

SAMUEL B. GOULD
Chancellor
University of California, Santa Barbara

PREFACE

College Student Government is the fourth revised edition of a United States National Student Association publication, *Student Leadership and Government in Higher Education,* which up to date has sold over fifteen thousand copies. The original editions were written by Gordon Klopf with the assistance of former members of the national staff of the association, Ralph A. Dungan, Jr., vice-president, and Richard Heggie, vice-president. Dr. Maurice Woolf, professor of education at Kansas State College, contributed to the section on student leadership for the third edition.

One of the new aspects of the present revision is a section for the student personnel and faculty advisers of student government and organizations. This was written in collaboration with Dr. Wilton Pruitt, acting dean of students, the State University of New York College of Education, Buffalo, New York.

The book does not aim to be the ultimate definition of the role of the student in the government of higher education but it does present a point of view which strongly urges that the student be given the opportunity to accept as much responsibility as he is able to in terms of his experience and the climate of the particular campus. It sees his student activity and student government participation as not only a democratic responsibility as a citizen of a college community but a laboratory for learning that is a very meaningful part of his college education.

The volume reviews various approaches to student government but does not present a summary of different programs or attempt to describe numerous examples of student government. It aims rather to deal with basic points of view and principles and one major illustration.

College Student Government begins with an exploration of the campus group and the role of the group member. A consideration is given to the function and role of leadership in student organizations and how student governments can plan leadership training programs.

The second part of the book deals with the participation of students in college government. Basic considerations for student government are given.

The final section of the book deals with the role of the faculty and personnel worker in student government and student organizations.

The writer has been a consultant at many campuses throughout this country and Asia and owes no small part of his thinking to the ideas that students themselves have set forth. The staff of the National Student Association, particularly Diane Hatch, executive vice-president; Fred Werner, student government vice-president; and Florence Casey, public-relations director have been of assistance in this revision.

The writer is deeply indebted to the students at the State University of New York College of Education in Buffalo and particularly to the personnel staff and faculty there for their continuous testing of some of his basic convictions.

The real support, both administrative and philosophical, came from Dr. Harvey Rice, president of Macalester College, and former president of the State University College in Buffalo. His real concern for the democratic process gave the writer and the students at Buffalo an opportunity to develop a very effective program of student participation in college administration in this country.

The graduate students and the staff of the Department of Guidance and Student Personnel Administration at Teachers

College, Columbia University, have explored many of the writer's ideas with him. No small appreciation goes to Mrs. Anne Williams, who typed the manuscript and has been of real assistance to the writer during the current revision.

GORDON KLOPF

Visiting Professor of Education
Teachers College
Columbia University
New York
    and
Dean of Students
College of Education
State University of New York
Buffalo, New York

I

Developing student leadership

The student and the group

The presence of a wide variety of student groups is a characteristic of most American college campuses. These range from highly organized to spontaneous and unorganized groups. Although this book will deal with the development of leadership in organized groups and the planning of purposeful student governments, the nonstructured groups on the campus are important to the student and are significant elements in the folkways and mores of the campus. The residence hall corridor bull session, the campus hangout cliques, friends who get together to eat, students walking around the quadrangle together, and the behind-the-scenes non-office holding power group in a fraternity are examples of groups which do have real influence on the student and his development.

Although extensive research has not been done to support the belief that participation in activities does have value for the student and is a vital part of his total education, it is the belief of many educators that student activities have positive values for the college student.

Being a member of a group gives a student status and acceptance as well as opportunities for fellowship and comradeship. Many of these group experiences can be learning

experiences in human relations and understanding human behavior. Through sharing responsibility for group progress and
programs he learns the skills of participating effectively in
groups and leadership. Concepts of democracy and citizenship
roles can become live and dynamic phenomena rather than
textbook theories.

Cultural activities help to broaden his sensitivities to the
richness of life and the world's heritage. Sports and recreational
activities provide relaxation and physical exercise. Service
groups help him to see needs beyond those of his own. Social
groups meet his great desire for belonging. Religious activities
can provide avenues for gaining religious maturity.

Recent studies show the importance of the college community in influencing the values of the student. Group participation can develop shallow values and undesirable traits
unless students and faculty give real thought to the student
government and activity programs on campuses. Democratic
concepts and leadership do not just naturally result from
participation. Students can learn to be authoritarian, benevolent, and manipulative leaders. They can use the status which
activities give them for escape from academic responsibilities.
Confined social group membership can develop feelings of
class superiority.

If it is assumed that participation in group life on the campus
is a significant factor in higher education, then boards of
trustees, presidents, administrators, faculty members, and students themselves must accept the responsibility for providing
the most meaningful and significant student activities and student government programs that are possible.

How groups develop

Fundamental to learning concepts of leadership is the development of an understanding of the group itself, how it develops
and the importance of participant roles within it. At the start

all groups are basically just collections of individuals, whether they are faculty, student, or community organizations. Groups may remain as such during their entire existence or the individuals within them may work together for the development of mature working units. As groups grow from collections of individuals, the members have to understand themselves, and do so in relationship to the group and its objectives and purposes. At first every member will assert himself and attempt to secure status through behavior which may at times be like that of the unsocialized infant. Intercommunication between members of the group may also be poor in the early stages of the life of a group.

Gradually shifts from concern for self to the purpose of the organization will take place. Hostile, emotionally-toned behavior becomes group- and work-centered. The individuals will see the group objectives as well as their own and will begin to share group tasks with the leader. The leader will not have the full responsibility for the group's function, but instead each member will assume his share to enable the group to function well. Each member, as well, becomes more interested in the ideas and productivity of others in the group, he accepts responsibility for the operation and functioning of the group, and has less concern for his own energetic and personal needs.

As groups mature they have less difficulty in reaching decisions, their discussions become more thorough and complete, fewer personality clashes and emotional reactions are evident, and skill is gained in ability to move from decision to action.

Less competition is present in productive organizations. Co-operative rather than competitive interrelationships improve the intercommunication between the members, the co-ordination of effort, the friendliness and pride in the group, and the general basic harmony and effectiveness of the group. The individual must develop a sensitivity to his own needs and motivations as well as to those of others in the group.

Improving group member roles

Student groups vary. The individuals in them have unique personal needs; the group itself differs from others in its stage of readiness, backgrounds, and resistance to change. However, if the organization is to grow and be productive as a group, individuals need to share experiences and respect the contributions of others.

A great deal of emphasis is given to the role of the leader and little has been said about the participant's actual role. Groups need to have leaders who perform co-ordinating, initiating, organizing, expediting, mediating, and encouraging roles. However, participants in the groups need to be more than followers. Actually leadership is a shared responsibility. Every member performs a task which will help the group in its productivity and progress. Members must assume their share of leadership functions.

In understanding roles that individuals assume in groups it is necessary to recognize that the tasks performed in a group are associated with the personalities of the individuals involved. The cultural, social, and economic background, their previous club and organization experiences, and their whole personality structure will partially determine the role they serve in the group. For example, an individual with hostile feelings toward a member of the group or several members may block any contribution these individuals may attempt to make. Here the individual is using the group to satisfy individual needs and places his own concerns ahead of those of the group.

Basic needs of individuals determine the roles they play in an organization. Individuals want security, social approval, and vocational success. Members of the group must help each other meet these needs. Not only needs but also the motivating factor behind the individual's joining the group will determine his role in the group.

This might be described as "individual centered" participation. Kenneth Beene and Paul Sheats describe these "individual centered" roles as:[1]

1. The "aggressor"—may talk too much, deflates others, attacks the group's solutions, may think he has all of the answers.
2. The "blocker"—generally negativistic, disagrees and opposes ideas or individuals.
3. The "recognition seeker"—attempts to call attention to himself or his own ideas or projects, refers constantly to personal experiences.
4. The "self-confessor"—takes advantage of the group to express personal feelings, and ideas which may not necessarily be related to the group's objectives.
5. The "playboy"—seeks group attention but yet is not involved in the group's discussions or procedures through cynicism, nonchalance, horseplay—"out of field" behavior.
6. The "dominator"—asserts authority either directly or indirectly may flatter others to get their support or may be outright authoritative in his behavior.
7. The "help-seeker"—attempts to secure sympathy from other members of the group.
8. The "special interest pleader"—attempts to get group support for his own cause.

Individuals may not assume the same one of these "individual centered" roles in all groups. The social behavior of the individual depends upon the group, its purposes, its setting, and its personnel. A student may be a dominator in one group and

[1] *Kenneth D. Beene and Paul Sheats, "Functional Roles of Group Members,"* Journal of Social Issues, *Vol. IV., No. 2, Spring 1948, p. 41-49.*

in another situation be very shy and quiet. Individual and personal goals should not take precedence over group needs. For group maturity individual goals must be supplemented by group oriented goals.

To enable the group to progress there are a number of roles that individuals need to assume. These are productive roles rather than egocentric, personal roles. Individuals need to train themselves to react in terms of group standards rather than individual needs.

The most common productive role that a member may assume is that of the individual who seeks or gives opinion or, sometimes called the "information giver," "the opinion giver," the "information seeker," and "the opinion seeker."

The "elaborator" is one who helps the group to approach a problem more intensively. In addition to the co-ordinating done by the chairman, members may also serve as "co-ordinators." In this role they clarify relationships and bring together ideas of various members of the group. The person who helps the group expedite its procedures may be called the "procedural technician." He may take the roll, arrange a display, distribute materials, or make announcements.

Group members also need to serve as "energizers" and "encouragers" to arouse and stimulate the group. "Harmonizers" and "compromisers" are also useful to serve as mediators and to relieve tension and conflict. The group member must compromise when his own ideas and plans are involved and serve as a "harmonizer" when others are in disagreement.

These productive roles are not played consistently by the same person. Group members assume those roles which will enable the group to solve problems quickly, to plan activities efficiently, and to have good discussions. They must become sensitive to needed group roles and become proficient in different roles. Groups in different stages of development have different role requirements. For example, early in the discussion of a problem, the role of information seeker and giver is frequently important. To become a productive group the members will have to assume the role which they think will best serve the needs of the group, but not hold back from reflecting their own ideas, concerns, and convictions.

Concepts of leadership

Through the years a number of concepts of leadership have evolved. One of the commonly accepted theories is that leadership is something which resides within a person who has certain personality and behavior traits. Proponents of this school of thought might even say that leaders are born not made. Another point of view that has developed more recently is that leadership is a phenomenon closely related to the situation or the group in which the leader functions. Different situations and groups call for different types of leadership roles and behavior. Some current thinking may be considered to combine elements of both of these concepts, as Gouldner states:[2] The leader is any individual whose behavior stimulates patterning of the behavior in a group. A concept of shared leadership sees the opportunity for this behavior given to any member of the group. It may be an interaction between the group and any one member.

One must relate these concepts of leadership behavior in groups with the behavior of the elected, appointed, or designated leader who is known as the president or chairman of an organization. The individual in the position of leadership needs to have as his basic aim, as Gordon[3] says, the tapping and developing of the creative resources of his group members. He needs to believe in the sharing of his leadership functions.

Leadership is a social phenomenon. Although there are

[2] *A. W. Gouldner, (ed.)* Studies in Leadership. (*New York: Harper & Brothers, 1950), p. 17.*

[3] *Thomas Gordon,* Group Centered Leadership. (*New York: Houghton Mifflin Co., 1955), p. 8.*

certain types of leaders, the role the student leader plays is always determined by his own personality and the particular setting in which he is functioning.

Maurice Woolf has described four basic types of leaders: the "hard-boiled" autocrat; the benevolent autocrat; the laissez-faire leader; the democratic leader. Student leaders may not classify into one of these four categories, but they may follow a general behavior pattern which varies with the situation in which they are assuming the leadership role.

The "hard-boiled" autocrat attempts to achieve his goals by giving orders, assigning tasks, making decisions without consulting the group, and checking up periodically to see if the work is being done. He does not trust others, hence the constant supervision of those under him. Part of the technique is to bow and scrape to those above him in the hierarchy of power. Power in this case usually comes from above and can be imposed on the group. Discipline is maintained through fear of punishment. The group has a prescribed responsibility to carry out decisions and is discouraged from thinking creatively. The leader, of course, has to take a maximum responsibility for the performance of the group and oftentimes the group feels a certain amount of security on this account. They know what to expect, how far they can go. People react generally in one of three ways to this kind if leadership. (1) They become submissive and dependent. They are able to rationalize their situation and accept their follower role without resentment. (2) They become openly hostile and express resentment and fight for reform. (3) They feel hostile and turn this into a depression and lack of hope for the future.

The benevolent autocrat knows what is best for his people. He has a soft manner, lets the group know that he has their interests at heart, that he is willing to sacrifice for them, reasons carefully with them to bring them around to his point of view. He does this by presenting alternatives. Always his ideas are in the best light and no one with wisdom would choose the poor alternative. He is seldom harsh or severe. He seldom delegates power or responsibility. He likes to trade benevolence for loyalty. He praises people when they agree with him. He has no twinge of conscience about withholding information from the group, and may disregard information that isn't in agreement with his plans. He likes people to be dependent on him and seek his advice. The group gets confused without knowing why. The leader will say, "We want to find out what everybody thinks about this," or "We want to be democratic about this," but the action of the leader doesn't square with his talk and as a result there is loss of motivation in the group, a resigned submissiveness, and apathy.

The laissez-faire leader seldom offers a suggestion to his group. Everyone is free to express himself. He makes information or materials available. He makes no attempt to clarify issues nor does he ask for an evaluation of the work of the group or the process that is going on. He has no clear-cut ideas of the goals of the group. The group is likely to wander aimlessly on the subject under discussion. He is likely to give special privilege in order to be a "good fellow." He is unwilling to destroy the cordiality of an interpersonal relationship and, therefore, unable to be aggressive. He is just the opposite of the hard-boiled autocrat and this is the reason why many people confuse laissez-faire leadership with democratic leadership.

Under lassez-faire leadership very little gets accomplished and the group loses morale and may fall apart. Laissez-faire leadership permits anarchy since any person or persons are permitted to do about as they please.

The democratic leader really believes in the ability of his group to explore problems or issues, discuss them freely without fear, and arrive at sensible decisions and conclusions. He believes every one should have the opportunity to contribute to the solution of problems confronting the group. He uses his position to co-ordinate the work of the group, to keep them oriented toward group goals, and to use all the resources of the group. He does this by defining the situation—clarifying issues—bringing together the threads of thought expressed by the group, sometimes asking for compromise and occasionally offering suggestions. He is wary about minorities using special strategy to accomplish their ends and calls on the group observer to make comments about actions that facilitate group progress and those that hold it up.

At all times he wants full and adequate discussion of issues and thorough understanding of them. He does not want a few to do all the talking. He knows that people who have axes to grind and influence to peddle are not always oriented toward group goals.

Characteristics of this group are independent thought, consideration for varying points of view, respect for the opinions and work of every member, progress toward goals and action following group decisions. Since his followers have the power of decision, they, therefore, have to take the responsibility for their action—right or wrong.

The democratically administered group seems to lead in work enthusiasm, quality, and quantity of production. The leader endeavors, where possible, to share with his group decision making about work planning, assignment, and scheduling. Where a decision must be made by him, he does it in terms of policy set up by the group or by group precedent; and if there is none he helps the group to understand clearly his basis for decision. He helps the group to develop an objective attitude about its work and ways of testing its own thinking.

The democratic leader presupposes that every man possesses a certain amount of dignity, and that this dignity should be honored by giving him equal opportunity to speak, work, etc., that each individual achieve status (it is not given nor assigned to him) according to his innate ability, opportunity, and work. He also assumes that there is a small cluster of tendencies in the human make-up that is basically social. These tendencies cause the individual to be sensitive to, and to depend upon, others. The most important of these seems to be the inclination to enjoy the feeling of "belongingness" (derived from participation), and to desire to talk things over. These are both highly important to the success of group action. Around these two in particular seems to develop much of the patterning of interpersonal feelings in the group. Much of the success of the person in the leader role depends upon his capitalization, for the group, upon these social tendencies.

The success of this method of leadership depends not only on the techniques used by the leader but also on his ability to communicate his feeling toward the people in his group both by word of mouth and by action. The group must feel the integrity of their leader and that the will of the leader:

1. Is committed to the goals of the group.
2. Has faith in the ability of the group.
3. Insists on free expression of ideas even though they are opposite to his own.
4. Is fair and honest in the handling of all questions.
5. Does not take away any of their powers.
6. Develops leadership ability within the group.

Most leaders can be placed on a hypothetical scale with the conservatives at one end and the radicals at the other. The conservatives want to preserve the status quo and look to the past for their quest. Some would like to re-establish the past. The radicals want to revolutionize things immediately and are willing to indulge in violence. In the middle of the scale you find the liberal, who wants change but wants it to be orderly and peaceful. He looks toward the future, has in mind change

in terms of equal opportunity and basic human rights for all.
Every leader knows that bringing about change is sometimes hazardous. Change involves the unfreezing of certain
principles, ideas, mores, customs, laws, making certain modi-
fications, and then freezing them at another level. During this
process, clubs, student government groups, and other organizations try to ascertain if they will derive as much benefit
from the change as they would from the old order. Some institutions are always threatened by proposed change and their
reactions are defensive and oftentimes hostile. The leader,
therefore, has to be able to deal with hostility in a group and
hold it to a minimum. Telling the individuals or factions within
a group how they feel about the issue helps. They feel better
understood and less hostile when this is done. It relieves the
tension enough so that the participants can be more objective
in making their comments.

Evaluating group progress

In its process of growth and development the student organization needs to evaluate its progress as a group.

A group will also find it necessary to understand its own
objectives and functions through a thorough discussion of its
history, constitution, and future plans. When these are clarified, the group may utilize fully the contributions of all members in achieving the set goals. Interest-indicator cards or
personal interviews will give the group's leaders an insight
into the interests and abilities of the group members. The
organization will also be able to determine whether the abilities
of the group are so limited that additional resources must be
brought in to help serve its function. The organization adviser
can frequently be of assistance in helping a group to learn
what its limitations and strengths are.

The students in a residence hall on a New England campus

held a leadership conference and came to the following conclusions concerning standards for group effectiveness:

 a) The group is most effective when all of the members
 are involved in the entire process, from planning through
 to the execution and evaluation. This involvement, to be
 real, necessitates that the activity be of importance to the
 members and that they feel that the results of their efforts
 will be meaningful to themselves, and to others.
 b) The group is most effective when all members actively
 participate and make their unique contributions. This full
 participation depends somewhat upon the degree of involvement described above and also upon the leader of
 the group. The leader must expect all to contribute and
 accept all efforts with respect. He must develop skill in
 helping the group to do likewise.
 c) The group is most effective when it has within its
 membership, or can call upon, resource persons representing all points of view and especially those that contribute
 insight and perspective.[4]

One of the means of studying its process is to have the group
do some "role playing." In "role playing" several individuals
act out before the group problem situations which are preventing group progress. Role playing should not last more
than ten minutes in a small, informal group. If the technique
is used as a demonstration device before an audience, it might
last considerably longer.

The student leader should utilize the role-playing situation
to stimulate discussion concerning the behavior of the group.
Frequently role playing can become a humorous situation
rather than a living experience. If the leader or the group
desires to use the technique, he must approach it seriously.

[4] *Edith Wilson,* Using Group Dynamics in the Residence Halls," *Journal
of the National Association of Deans of Women, Vol. XV, No. 3, March
1952, p. 126.*

The evaluation of meetings is a device which can help organizations to ascertain how they are functioning. Various forms of end-of-the-meeting evaluation or rating sheets are described in the books listed in the bibliography. The following questions are some which might be asked of a group after a meeting. The summary of these ought to be given at the next meeting and should be presented with a discussion of the implications and observations.

GROUP PROGRESS:

1. How far did the group go in any particular direction during a particular period?

2. Did all of the members understand where they were going and what they were trying to do?

3. Was progress halted by a lack of information?

4. Did the group wander and stray from the adopted agenda? If so, was it with agreement of the members?

GROUP UNITY:

1. Was everyone equally interested in what the group was trying to do?

2. Did the group begin to subordinate individual interests and experiences to common goals and problems?

3. Was the general atmosphere of the group formal or informal?

4. Did the delegates feel free to express themselves or did the environment lack casualness and inhibit discussions?

5. Was there a feeling of cooperation and friendliness or competitiveness and hostility?

CONTRIBUTION OF THE LEADER:

1. Did the leader have a tendency to dominate?

2. Did the leader try to help the group draw conclusions and make generalizations?

3. Did the leader work with the group in developing

ideas and plans rather than telling them what they were to do and how they were to do it?

4. Did the leader serve as a source of information when it was needed?

5. Did the leader help the group evaluate how they were working together?

6. Did the leader permit the leadership to be assumed by other individuals in the group?

CONTRIBUTION OF GROUP MEMBERS:

1. Did everyone participate or did a few monopolize the discussion?

2. Did individual members have a tendency to stray from the subject being discussed?

3. Did each individual make his contribution, build on and add to the contributions of the previous speakers?

4. Did the delegates actually listen to each other's comments or were they more concerned about what they were going to say next?

5. Did individuals make their contributions rise above a personal and emotional level?

Training for leadership

EMERGING STUDENT LEADERSHIP—It is generally accepted by educators that leadership can be learned. However, leadership is understood as a set of functions performed within a group. Therefore, more than just the student leader must be trained; the club, organization, and committee members, whatever the group may be, need training as well. Basic to the training of leaders is the necessity of giving the group members the tools with which to help their group to grow.

Students must be given opportunities to assume responsibility in the college scene if they are going to develop leadership. The responsibilities must be related to the actual functioning of the college as well as in those areas usually thought of as student activities.

A progression of experiences helps the student leader to gain the understanding necessary for assuming major positions of leadership. Most real student leaders have "come up through." They have experienced leadership at all levels, and have worked on committees, in clubs, and have shown leadership in the classroom. The experiences they seek are not just experiences but opportunities for the development of skills and techniques of group leadership as well as an understanding of human relations. Leadership develops most extensively in meeting new situations, and the student who avoids excessive duplication of positions of leadership has a greater opportunity to grow.

He evaluates a particular activity in terms of the experience that it will give to him as well as the interest he has in it. In this regard he recognizes that each activity may have something different to offer.

Thus, participation in team athletics develops both the student's physical co-ordination and his abilities to think quickly and to work with others under fire. Participation in a subcommittee of student government or related council provides experience in carrying out small responsibilities and in co-operating with others for common goals. The chairmanship of such a committee gives practical training in administration and delegation of responsibility as well as in the leading of problem-solving discussions. A member of the student governing body receives, in addition, the wider experiences of representing the opinions of others, participating in parliamentary debates, and helping to form policy for the students as a whole. Most of the officers have the opportunity to increase further their poise and maturity of thinking in their capacities of representing students before the public through the media of speeches, community committees, and similar agencies.

THE LEADERSHIP CONFERENCE—One of the most successful means of developing student leadership is to have an organized training program. The main feature of the program would be a campus leadership conference, or workshop.

A leadership workshop or conference differs from other types of conferences in that it is basically a training experience. Many student conferences which deal with campus issues and programs are held. These have as their purpose the studying or exploration of problems with the hope that some useful conclusions will be reached or resolutions drawn at the conference. Frequently, student conferences have both training aspects and programs dealing with student issues and problems. If a conference time period is sufficiently long, the two may be done effectively. However, if the time allotted for the conference is only a week end, it is best to differentiate the two and, in a leadership training week-end session, have no more than one short block of time dealing with campus issues.

The time of the conference varies with campus needs, calendars, and the time of campus elections. Some colleges find it most satisfactory to have the conference in the late spring and others prefer to have it at the beginning of the fall semester. Perhaps the most satisfactory method is to have conferences both semesters with one of them being more extensive than the other.

It has generally been found best to have a leadership conference at a location that is not on the college campus or too close to it. Youth camps, small hotels or inns, or other public outing or recreational grounds that are self-contained and house only one group are the ideal places for student leadership training conferences. If the weather is satisfactory and the facilities are adequate these locations usually provide good recreational facilities and a pleasant, informal atmosphere.

Participants to the conference should be limited to from a hundred to a hundred and twenty-five. They ought to be drawn from incoming and outgoing student officers. Students who would just like to come and are not in a position of leadership ought to have the opportunity to be able to do so to a limited degree. Faculty should be encouraged to participate and can best be involved as resource persons or discussion leaders. They ought to serve a more meaningful role than chaperones.

It would seem that the student government might be the most effective sponsoring agency for the conference but in appointing the planning committee consideration is given to all points of view and interests on the campus. The planning committee should not be just representatives or members of the student government. Someone who is concerned professionally with leadership training and group development, either on the staff of the student personnel program or in the sociology, psychology and education departments might serve as an adviser or consultant to the planning committee. If no one is available on the campus, there may be individuals in community organizations who can provide this counsel.

If a campus has never had a leadership training program the level of sophistication at which the program begins will be different from what it would have been if there had been a series of programs through the years. However, even though a series of conferences has been sponsored it is important that the core group does not become too erudite, and "ingroupish" in the theory of group leadership. If they use too much of the jargon and reflect too much sophistication, those who have not been attending the conferences regularly will find it difficult to participate in the group. It is also essential that if a campus has never sponsored a leadership training conference, professional assistance be used to a greater degree. As students work with conferences year after year they should be able to assume training functions themselves.

The planning group will find it very helpful to read Pro-

fessor Matthew Miles book, *Learning To Work in Groups*.[5]
In his volume he urges that the logical order of content for a
leadership training program be: (1) the history of group development, of group dynamics; (2) general characteristics of
groups; (3) the nature of leadership; (4) membership responsibility in groups; and (5) personality in group work.[6]

Just how content is presented and how "skill learning" in
group leadership takes place may be approached in various
ways. Informed and knowledgeable faculty members or outside consultants may provide content through talks, panels and
films, and printed materials. These may be supplemented by
buzz groups, small group discussions or large group discussions.

Further learning and adaptation of content takes place
through role playing and the discussions of typical cases. Role
playing is successful if the members approach the assigned
issue, situation, or problem seriously and interpret the roles
with their keenest perception. There needs to be a discussion
led by someone in a training capacity after the role playing to
point up and clarify the behavior and issues. Case studies provide the opportunity for the students to look at a situation
quite objectively. The planning committee will find real
learning experience in writing the case studies to be used in
the discussion groups.

The small groups are the heart of the conference. They
should not exceed fifteen in the number of participants. The
leader should help the group get acquainted with one another
by asking for self-introductions. He should help the group to
determine its problems without influencing the planning. An
agenda is an important tool with which he can assist the group
to guide its discussion. He should also give guidance in helping
it to reach conclusions to be presented to the general sessions.
Not only should issues be dealt with in broad terms but in

[5] *Matthew B. Miles*, Learning To Work in Groups. *Bureau of Publications,
Teachers College, Columbia University; New York, 1959.*

[6] Ibid., *p. 85.*

specific situations as well. The experiences of each participant should be considered as the issues are considered. The group leader serves chiefly to help clarify questions, to make sure that there is maximum participation, to ask thought-provoking questions, to restate unclear points, to help participants distinguish facts from conjectures, and to encourage a good feeling in the group. The leader should not attempt to answer questions introduced by members in the group; he should refer them to other participants. If only one point of view is introduced, he might help the group search for different approaches to the problem. If conflicts arise, he should try to help the group discover the main issues and how to resolve them.

The discussion group as well as the general sessions will need a recorder to keep a written record of the group's thinking. Many conferences have found it helpful to appoint a group observer as well. The observer is someone who helps the group to evaluate its progress. If an observer is not used, the chairman should help the group to evaluate itself. Is it really functioning as it should? Is it reaching some conclusions? Is everyone participating in the discussion? These are just a few of the possible questions the leader can ask the group to think about.

The whole setting of the conference is important to its success. The rooms used by discussion groups should have tables or chairs that are arranged in a circle or square so that each participant can see the others. If the students do not know each other, participants should wear name cards or have them in front of them on the table. There should be a blackboard and other equipment which the group may want to use. The location of the conference ought to have available one large room for general sessions, films, and any large group social activities. The use of a fireplace around which there might be a late evening sing, a floor that can be used for square dancing, Ping-pong tables, and other recreational facilities all help to make for high morale at a conference.

Students may want some sessions at a leadership conference

dealing with some of the specific problems they have in their organizations. Some of these technique clinics, or orientation sessions might be in the area of social activity planning, publicity methods, parliamentary law, how to conduct large meetings, how committees function, the role of the faculty adviser, the use of films, how to lead discussions, how to plan programs using community resources, and how to initiate group action. These sessions might be led by a student chairman with a student or faculty member presenting some initial points of view or information, followed by discussions. It is certainly helpful at these workshops if there are some illustrative materials to distribute. For example, if you are discussing a role of the treasurer in student organizations, there are certain policies or procedures which the college requires of treasurers. Copies of this material ought to be available for the members of the training group.

After an initial leadership conference at a college has been held, succeeding conferences might deal with additional concepts and skills. A conference might explore more specifically the techniques of problem solving, using role playing and case discussions dealing with the presentation of the theory of problem solving. A conference might deal more specifically with roles that individuals play in groups. It might place some emphasis on the individual and how his particular personality, make-up and background is affected by the group and affects the group. This latter type of emphasis which deals with a good deal of personal diagnosis requires sensitivity and skill. It is in this type of program the students will need a good deal of professional resource assistance.

After a conference is over, the planning committee will want to hold an evaluation session. Some type of evaluation sheet or questionnaire should be given to the participants and the results should be tabulated. One of the major criteria for evaluating a conference should be the degree to which the participants were involved in discussion, in problem solving sessions, and the general session.

Dr. Matthew Miles recommends the use of occasional Hollywood films which focus on group situations. Among those suggested are:

Twelve Angry Men	United Artists
Executive Suite	M.G.M.
Lifeboat	20th Century-Fox
Home of the Brave	United Artists
All the Kings Men	Columbia

These not only provide an opportunity for recreation but good content for follow-up discussion.

No leadership conference will have permanent value unless it is followed by a continuing training program. The theory and skills of group leadership cannot be learned in two or three days at a college camp. A series of seminars might follow during the college year. A number of colleges have very successfully held weekly seminars dealing with group development and group leadership. At these weekly seminars the students gain a great deal of skill and insight and become the core group for the training week-end conference. They also serve as consultants to student organizations who are seeking help with some of their problems. Some campuses require individuals running for campus offices to take a short course in group leadership sponsored by the student government.

Another means of developing student leadership is the reading of literature in the field of group activities. Many national organizations publish handbooks, magazines, and other materials that are helpful to officers and chairmen. Some of the books concerning student organizations, group process, group leadership are listed at the end of this booklet. There is an increasing number of effective films which can be used at conferences or on the campus during the year for follow-up training sessions. These are also listed at the end of this book.

II

Student participation in college administration

The historical development

The traditional label for the activities which students develop relative to the role they play in the governing of the college is "student government." Student participation in college government is neither a novelty nor a modern idea, even though in the United States it has flourished largely during the past few decades. The practice of having students responsible for and exercising control over their conduct and activities extends over a period of many centuries. Educational historians point out that the early practices of permitting students to control themselves were not conscious processes of education and as such do not completely coincide with our present concepts of student government as a valuable educational experience.

"Student government" in the Middle Ages developed from a genuine need on the part of students. Scholars came from foreign lands and were thrown on their own resources. Because of oppression they were forced to form "nations" or guilds for their own protection. These organizations first appeared during the latter part of the twelfth century. In no other university did they acquire so much prestige or power as they did at the University of Paris. It was from here that the idea of guilds spread throughout Europe and into England.

The organization of such governing groups on a national level found its most rapid development in Italy because of the peculiar political and civil disunity that was characterstic of that period in Italian history. Since the foreign students enjoyed no political rights they were forced to unite in order to exercise effectively the reputations that they had gained in the towns.

Another important development of student self-governing groups came with the advent of crowded houses or dormitory halls which required some sort of management. At first this task was undertaken by the students. They formed a democratic community and selected a principal. In time the principal was vested with certain powers by the university and the form changed from one of republicanism to monarchism. A few survivors of these halls or hospitas, as they were called, still remain at Oxford and Cambridge.

The character of self-government which distinguished universities of the Middle Ages showed itself in various ways. It was indicated in the principle of the choice of officers, the brief duration of the powers conferred, and in the eminently honorary nature of those powers. The real seat of action lay in the general assembly of the university or in the particular assemblies of the nations or faculties. Generally, the rector became the prime scholastic power in the university; his other powers varied widely in the different institutions. At the University of Bologna the rector had to be a student and under twenty-five years of age. The assembly which the rector headed usually consisted of representatives from the nations. An issue would be discussed initially at the assembly, and the final decision made at the General Assembly. In many of the universities the teachers had their own organizations in the form of faculties which were often represented in the assemblies as well. Student government in the medieval university was essentially different from our present form in that a pressing social and economic need lay at the base of the medieval organization, while in America it arose as the application of a democratic ideal to education.

Student government has also developed in the United States as a result of students wanting a means of organizing and channeling their opinion concerning programs, services, issues, fees, and charges, particularly those areas which affect student welfare. Student government is also seen by student personnel workers as a means of teaching not only citizenship skills but effective human relations and group procedures.

The development of student government in this country has come slowly, because of the grip of the German scholastic and research tradition on American educational thinking. Many native educators, during the eighteenth and nineteenth centuries, received a great part of their training in Germany and were greatly influenced by the philosophies of the German system. German educators, concentrating on the teaching of facts, had little concern for the individual's competence to accept social responsibilities. Not only was there no self-government in the German institution, but also there was little or no organized provision for social life, recreation, shelter, food, and employment for those who could not afford college.

In the United States, formalistic classroom student-teacher relationships of the Germanic concept of objectivity were partially countered by the idealism of Thomas Jefferson and the informal tradition of British dormitory life. But many a continental-trained professor and those taught by them have continued to demonstrate either opposition to, or complete distrust in the ability of students to manage their affairs outside the classroom, and thereby have resisted the giving of governing responsibility to the student.

The paternalistic role of the administration and governing boards of colleges may also have prevented the growth of student government. Administration and concerns of control and government were best handled by agencies and individuals who were not students. Little study has been made of the value systems of earlier generations of students but prior to the thirties and forties it might be assumed that their interests and concerns were more social than citizenship-oriented. It was during these years that the fraternity system made its initial great strides. A policy of tolerance of student groups rather than an administrative philosophy of working with them to achieve educational goals during the early years of higher education in America could also be a reason why student government groups did not develop. The popularity of the debating and public speaking societies may have met the needs of those students who had concern for political activities and citizenship roles.

Some form of student government has been apparent in American colleges since the late 1700's when William and Mary College organized a student governing body. With the founding of the University of Virginia, Jefferson recommended a modified plan of student discipline, and since that time many other institutions have claimed that American student government was founded on its campus. Although early attempts were fraught with failure, the seeds were sown.

Jefferson's ideas of student government were advanced and his main thesis was that it should provide a training in citizenship. Experiments were tried along these lines by Trinity, Yale, Oberlin, and Union colleges. During the period following 1870, many more attempts were made, including those at the universities of Illinois, South Carolina, and Amherst, to provide student government of some type. Not a few failed because they leaned too far to the extremes. On the one hand the system has failed because a large amount of power was given to students with little faculty or administration guidance and the students were unable to handle the powers. On the other hand too little power was given or too close supervision was maintained, leading to student government in name only.

The National Self-Government Committee, Inc., an organization led by Richard Welling, wielded some influence in higher education in the development of concepts of student government in the 1920's and 1930's. The National Student Federation of the United States of America, a loosely knit federation of student governments functioning during the thirties, met annually and discussed the organization and principles of student government.

Basically the first half of the twentieth century saw student government evolve on most American campuses, but its function has been chiefly that of supervision of student social activities. The Intercollegiate Association of Women Students has done much to stimulate interest in women's student government. With the organization of the National Student Association in 1946, student government was given a tremendous impetus. The mature veteran students were interested in having a voice in the governing of their affairs and student governing groups flourished.

As a result of this great upsurge of interest in student government, the exploration of the student's role in the government of the college initiated several studies in the ensuing ten years. The National Student Association has distributed a series of mimeographed pamphlets concerning student government and leadership. A summary of some loosely structured questionnaires on student leaders, *Student Government, Student Leaders and the American College*, edited by E. Friedson, was also published by the association in 1955. Another document which deals with some original material and some of the observations in the Friedson study, *The Student's Role in College Policy Making*, by H. Lunn, was issued by the American Council on Education in 1957. The Bureau of Publications of Teachers College, Columbia University, published, *Student Participation in College Administration*, by Frances Falvey in 1954.

Although no studies have been done to support the conclusion that meaningful student governments are increasing in American colleges, there are many evidences of what seems to be a rather phenomenal growth. The number of workshops, seminars, and publications dealing with leadership and student activities has increased. The National Student Association's Student Government Information Service cannot keep up with the requests for information. National professional college personnel associations are including in their annual conventions more programs each year dealing with student government. The unusually large sale of the three editions of this publication alone is some evidence of growth and interest.

In many institutions the role of student government will perhaps always remain as that of dealing with student activities. Some colleges may add various conduct and honor system responsibilities. But as higher education progresses in America, there will be more thought given to increasing the responsibility of the student in governing his college.

A point of view

If if is assumed that the college is a laboratory for training in citizenship, it might well be thought of as a community-structured unit. It must be remembered that a college has many characteristics which make it different from other types of communities. Its areas to govern are frequently delegated by other powers such as the state legislature, alumni, regents, and trustees. The campus community, Paul Brouwer[1] believes, is also one which is primarily educative in purpose, as well as one that is transitory in nature. Only too common is the campus that is a double-cultured group, the students with their mores and traditions, and the faculty with its patterns and customs.

[1] *Paul J. Brouwer*, Student Personnel Services in General Education. *(Washington, D.C.: The American Council on Education, 1949), p. 292.*

The American college community must work for a single-cultured standard, as Brouwer says, with students and faculty working together as members of a single community. The barriers between students and faculty must be lowered. The students not only need the experience of helping to frame the policies which will affect their lives while in college, but they should have some voice in the development of curriculum and in the evaluation of instruction.

Not only should students work with the faculty on committees and boards because students may have something to offer, but the students need the experience of working and planning with individuals who have had more experience than they as students have had. Governing groups need to deal with real issues and work closely with all ages and experience levels on the campus. Few vocational avenues in life are structured to one age group. To implement this the student needs not only to have extensive experiences with upperclassmen but in working with faculty and administrators as well.

The major areas that have been overlooked by both college adminstrations and students are the programs in which they should work closely together. Committees which deal with student affairs policies should have adequate student representation. Committees which are planning new curriculums or evaluating present curriculums should at least consult students for their opinions and ideas. College faculties and administrations should be constantly on the lookout for possible opportunities to expand the role of the student in administration.

Many avenues for student, faculty, administration cooperation are being experimented with today. One large institution has tried using a president's council with the president of the college meeting with ten or more of the key students as well as ten faculty members and administrators. Issues are discussed informally, but the administration really has the opportunity of learning how the students think and to incorporate their thinking in the development of the college policies. The students in turn can see the administration's point of view. Additional illustrations of types of student participation can be found in Lunn and Falvey.

One eastern college has students serving as either half or one-third of the membership of all the personnel committees with full voting power. The students in this institution also have seats with a vote on all of the government groups of the college. The representation and organization is as follows:

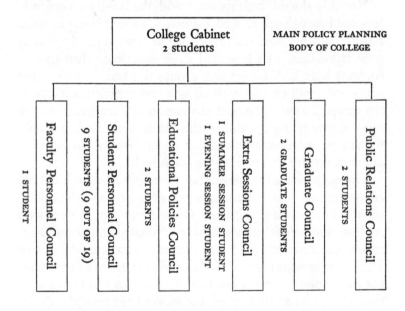

All the above councils have subcommittees on which from one to five students serve. The only exception is the Student Conduct Committee which has six students and three faculty members.

In evaluating the role that students have played in its policy-forming structure during the five-year period of operation the college has come to certain basic conclusions about student participation.

The *selection* of students who work on joint planning groups is extremely important. The appointment or selection method by the student congress is the best. The person must be interested in the assignment, have some background, and perhaps even some skill. He must believe in the particular area of concern. For example, if he is working on a curriculum committee he must be interested in it and believe in the importance of it. He also needs to have time.

Students who are going to work on joint committees as well as faculty need *orientation* to the committee. Students need to be introduced, need to have a meeting with the chairman as to the functions and goals of the committee. Faculty members, however, also need orientation to the concept of the student's role and really have to be amenable to the idea.

The students actually need to *share some of the responsibility equally*. If the committee is half composed of students, or includes one or two, they should have a vote. They need status and all of the privileges and rights of other members.

Discretion must be expected of students. In the writer's six years of experience with this integrated type of government, never once has a student released or discussed any information which might at the time have been considered confidential.

Communication is always a problem. What should the students report back to student government, to their friends, to other groups? How should they bring information that is organized and not their own highly personal opinion back to the central committee? This area needs to be studied carefully and clarified for student members.

It is important in developing this concept that the major administrators, or some power with recognizable status in the college community, believe in the concept of student participation. Although it is sometimes said that the chief administrator is not an influence in student government, the writer finds that it is difficult to have it function if there is not a sincere commitment on the part of some of the major administrators and some of the key faculty members.

Along with rights and privileges which the students share with faculty members, they must accept *responsibility*. This must be stated to them and, in most cases, they will follow through. If they can't come to meetings they will say so and ask to be excused. Because of the time and pressure perhaps one can't always expect the same role that one expects of a faculty member who is paid to serve this role. This has to be understood and the system cannot be condemned, because during exam time a student asks to be excused from attending a meeting.

The concept of the college as a community is basic to this whole approach to student participation in government. As Woodrow Wilson said,

> The College must become a community of scholars and pupils, a free community but a very real one in which democracy may work in reasonable triumphs and accommodation its vital process of union.

No better statement can be made in concluding this section than to quote Baker Brownell's definition of a community which needs to be applied as much as possible to the college community,

> The community is a group living under conditions in which people can know each other well. This knowing each other well includes work in face-to-face relationships. It includes diversified relationships as to age, sex, skill, function and mutual service to each other. It includes direct, cooperative relationships in many of the main activities of life and some sense of belonging, of solidarity. It involves, above all, a rather small group in which people

may know each other as whole persons rather than as functional fragments.[2]

The aims and objectives

The basic objective of students participating in the administration of an institution is to help them gain skills of citizenship. David Lilienthal once said that the core and essence of democracy is the participation of citizens in public affairs. The college community is the place where students must begin to participate in the affairs of their community and to assume some responsibility for it.

Experience in governing gives students a chance not only to learn the democratic processes but to experiment with them. Meaningful participation will develop mature individuals who recognize and respect their responsibilities for it.

An immediate purpose of student government is to provide a means whereby students may organize so as to be able to participate effectively in those functions of a college or university which directly affect their social, economic, physical, and intellectual welfare.

The degree to which they participate in the formation of policy or the actual implementation of it depends on the amount of authority granted to the governing body by the administration, the structure of the system, and the degree of their own interest.

The philosophy of the governing board and the president and/or other major administrator is a key factor in implementing student participation in college government. The dean of students who has a deep commitment to the concept can do a great deal to start the concept functioning by educating the president, the faculty, other administrators, and

[2] Baker Brownell, The College and the Community. (New York: Harper & Brothers, 1952), p. 10.

students to the many avenues of meaningful and creative learning it provides. There must be a basic belief in the student that he has not only a right but a real contribution to make in the development of college policy, goals, and programs. This means more than planning dances or handling campus traffic, although these have their place and function. Many administrators do not have a deep respect for the student and his contribution at whatever level of maturity and experience he has. They do not believe the student has something to contribute and that decisions which all share in making, and plans which develop after mutual consultation may be better decisions and plans than those which are developed alone. Where the student government is unable to participate in policy formation, it usually expresses student opinion when necessary, regardless of the amount of authority granted to it by the administration. This student expression sometimes takes the form of food riots, dorm raids, and demonstrations.

Among the primary functions of student government should be the co-ordination of all the student activities to make possible the maximum return to the entire educational community of students, faculty, and administration. Its constant aim must be one of service to the whole university else it has no purposeful existence.

The student on the American campus has long been noted for his boundless energy and abundant enthusiasm, which have all too seldom been channeled into activities which have befitted his dignity as a student or an individual. Therefore, it follows that when the question arises of allowing student agencies more responsibility, administration and faculty are apt to venture, "Oh, but they are too immature to use good judgment if we give them the authority." Might it not be well for them to ask themselves how responsibility in any walk of life can be taught without practical experience? Here it is necessary to re-emphasize that the method of trial and error is one which is

bound up with our whole educational process. Learning results
from experience as well as books and lectures.

Certainly practice in the university community, where mistakes can be corrected, is far better than carrying forth untested theories into the community where such mistakes are less tolerated and more disastrous. Healthful conformance to law is only the result of understanding its function, and it would appear that nowhere could more real understanding of the social and civil laws be taught than in our "communities" of higher learning.

Types of student participation

Although one might say that the number of forms of student governing groups is almost equal to the number of colleges which have self-government, it is relatively easy to break down existing forms into five categories: (1) community government; (2) the council; (3) the organizational council; (4) the bicameral government; (5) the association. In few instances do these exist in a pure form, for they are adapted to the situation on each campus. The organization may have legislative, judicial, executive, and administrative functions.

COMMUNITY GOVERNMENT—Community government in a college is generally composed of representatives from each group on the campus, administration, faculty, students, and sometimes business, clerical, and maintenance staff. It is truly a comprehensive organization of the whole institution. By its nature it is readily adaptable to student bodies of limited size, but in many respects becomes unwieldy when used in a large institution. Its theoretical basis is as close to the practical ideal of democracy as is possible. This form gives the greatest number direct share in the formation of policy. The complete community government system is not widely used in the United States, but has been employed effectively at a few colleges.

As has been indicated before, an institution can have the essence of the community type of college government if not the actual total structure, if there is an emphasis on including students on policy and administrative committees. Students in turn need to consult faculty members and to give them seats on their committees and councils.

The question is often asked on what committees students should be given seats. Although committee titles and responsibilities vary with institutions, the following are several which are found on most campuses and on which students could readily serve:

Orientation Committee
Admissions Committee
Lectures, Convocation and Chapel Committees
Athletic Committee
High School Relations Committee
Loans and Scholarship Committee
Housing Committee
Counseling Committee
Publications Committee
Social Committee
Commencement Committee
Educational Policy Committee

Curriculum Committee
Student Health Committee
Student Employment Committee
Student Personnel Committee
Library Committee
Student Affairs Committee
Student Conduct Committee
Public Relations Committee
Campus Planning Committee
Placement Committee
Student Activities Committee
Activities Eligibility Committee

Although opinions among educators differ, this writer believes that students should have faculty and administration represented on all their own committees and in the aspects of their student government structure which deal with broad campus issues and concerns. Recently a competent study of the library on a college campus was made by a student government library committee. However, when it was presented to the capable and yet sensitive director of the library it was not accepted. The report contained some excellent suggestions but the director felt it was critical and prepared without consideration of some of the financial and space limitations of the library. The student committee left the interview bitter and rejected. How much more effective it could have been if a team from the library staff and a group of students had worked together from the beginning of the study. When the students became aware of a need, they should have gone to the library director and consulted him from that point. The same holds true for student curriculum committees, faculty evaluation committees, food study surveys, and other student groups exploring areas with which they traditionally have little firsthand contact

THE STUDENT COUNCIL—The student council (nonorganizational) is so named because it is representative of the student body as a whole. In its purest form each member of the council is responsible to all the students and is elected by all the students. It is thus possible for him to maintain a broad and relatively objective outlook in his work.

One of the certain disadvantages attached to this type of government on a large campus is that each representative is far removed from the individual student since he is responsible to a large and perhaps amorphous group. Knowing that one personal opinion has little influence, many individual members of the electorate are apt to be unconcerned about who wins the elections and about what happens afterward—unless, of course, the council takes action obviously detrimental to their own welfare.

THE ORGANIZATIONAL COUNCIL—The organization or club council is made up of representatives of various campus organizations or groups. In its purest form each delegate on the council would be elected by the members of his group alone, and would be responsible chiefly to them.

It is usually composed of the heads of such campus organizations as debating clubs, dramatic socieites, glee clubs, fraternities, dormitories, etc. Many student governments have evolved from organizational councils, set up to co-ordinate the activities of the several groups represented.

This system insures the presence of specialists who will indeed be responsive to the interests of their electors. The chief difficulty is that they may be too responsive, and government may bog down as the result of the contentions of special interest groups. Questions which are not of direct concern to a group, on the other hand, are likely to be neglected by its representatives.

A further disadvantage arises out of the fact that all students may not be represented on the organizational council. Thus is it not a truly democratic body. If the attempt is made to make it more democratic by the inclusion of a greater number of representatives, the group is in danger of becoming unwieldly and inefficient.

The organization council may be a combination of several forms in an attempt to embody the advantages of both organizational and nonorganizational councils without retaining their weaknesses. There are so many variations of this form that it will be possible here only to outline the chief types.

A council may be based on academic group representation such as college class (year in school). It may be based on geographical areas in which students live. Such groupings have special interests but their interests may not interfere with the effectiveness of the student government to the extent that is true in the pure organizational council, since they constitute broader areas of concern.

A second type of combination system is the council on which students are represented both as a unit and as a series of units. On such a council there might sit delegates from the classes, delegates from the living groups, and representatives elected by the whole student body. On another such council the athletic associations, men's and women's associations, and various honor societies might be represented as well as the student body at large. The specific make-up depends on the tradition, organization, structure, and needs of the particular campus.

A third type of combination system is much like the second, the chief variation being that the organizational representatives have ex-officio status. The latter are present to offer comment and opinion under such a setup, but are not able to vote. A body thus constituted might have a disadvantage in that there are not enough organizations represented to give a well-rounded student opinion.

THE BICAMERAL GOVERNMENT—The bicameral government is one which is found on a few American campuses. It can embody either one or two of the forms previously mentioned. When it exists it is normally composed of an organ having both executive and legislative powers, and a larger assembly concerned strictly with legislation. Each body can check the other's action if it so desires, with the assembly possessing the ultimate authority.

The principal advantage of this system is that it provides opportunity for more students to participate in their campus government. It is possible, however, for the structure to become cumbersome and to result in indecisiveness or duplication.

Almost all the government forms discussed here have been in terms of a "council." There are many other titles applied to the highest student governing body, "council" being used here because it is the most common one. When the agency is known as a "senate," "legislature," or "legislative assembly," it generally denotes a larger group having primarily legislative functions. Such a group will likely fall into one of the categories of government outlined above.

THE STUDENT ASSOCIATION—An important factor to consider in student government is the relation of the governing board or council to the student body. Many student bodies should think of themselves as student associations and the student governing groups as the legislative council of the student association. Colleges that have student associations usually have some form of identification to give to the student to indicate that he is a member. This may be incorporated with the student activity fee card. On some campuses a student association fee is voluntarily solicited and only paid members are permitted to vote. On others a student pays an activity fee as part of his tuition and thus automatically becomes a member of the student association.

The five types of student government mentioned above refer to over-all centralized areas of student government. There are, in addition, many other phases of campus life which are self-governing and have governing boards and councils.

Representation in student governing groups

There are many theories of representation and the "ideal system" of representation in a democratic community. In writing constitutions students are faced with the problem of providing a system which will give full representation with respect to numbers and opinions and still provide a governing body of efficient size.

There is no set structure for representation. It varies with campuses and must be developed in terms of the individual student body and administrative structure. The following are some of the types of structure which are in general use.

THE WARD—The ward system provides for a geographic division of the campus and student living area and election of representatives from these areas, much the same as the prevailing municipal systems. Here the difference of representation may be generally well defined in terms of dormitory, fraternity, and boardinghouse areas. Here also, the advantage of having every student represented, organized or not, is quite apparent.

If the wards are fairly close-knit, there is ample opportunity for the representative to establish a close relationship with those whom he represents, and thereby to draw them into an active role in the life of the campus. If there is too great a degree of heterogeneity in each unit, however, there is a danger that the lack of group spirit will prevent adequate participation in elections and in the activities of student government.

THE LIVING GROUP—The living group system obtains representatives from organized students who share the same domicile. These include cooperative housing and dining groups, residence halls, fraternities, sororities, etc. This has the common failing of not representing the student who does not participate in a living situation, and of emphasizing the artificial divisions between each group.

CLASS REPRESENTATIVES—Representatives elected from a class have no distinguishing characteristics except their year in college and perhaps age. In some instances it might be said that they represent the particular interests of their class but sometimes these interests cannot be separated from those of the whole community.

This system can be most effective in drawing out the interest of students if there is a strong class spirit. The encouragement of friendly but competitive rivalries between classes is a very profitable method of encouraging enthusiasm over campus issues.

MEN'S AND WOMEN'S REPRESENTATIVES—Men's and women's associations or other key campus governing boards often supply representatives to student governing groups. The quality of such representation is obviously dependent upon the character of the association which supplies it. If these associations represent the whole campus and all students in a meaningful way, representatives from such groups can be desirable.

REPRESENTATIVES-AT-LARGE—Representatives-at-large sometimes constitute the student government in whole or in part. In this system delegates are chosen from the whole campus by the whole campus without any particular reference to representation of points of view caused by special, political, or economic stratifications. The advantages and disadvantages applicable here have already been enumerated.

SCHOOL, DIVISION OR COLLEGE DEPARTMENT REPRESENTATIVES —In a large university, schools or colleges are frequently the means for determining representation on the all-campus governing board and, in smaller colleges, departments or divisions. If the number on the board from each unit is partially decided on the basis of the enrollment, it can prove to be an excellent means of representation. Here again common aims and a certain degree of unity of thought among the members of each unit represented are necessary for the proper functioning of the government.

ORGANIZATION OR CLUB REPRESENTATION—Finally, there is the method of representation which is based on campus organizations which do not have living group characteristics but are members of student and professional groups. It is here that one finds the greatest discrepancies in numerical representation and the least in opinion representation.

THE POLITICAL PARTY—More frequently than not a campus uses a combination of the above means of representation. The basis for selection of a system or combination of systems should be in terms which will represent most effectively the greatest number of students.

At those institutions where no electoral method seems to bring the student closer to his government, there is another means which can be utilized for this purpose: the campus political party. A party system, if formed on a foundation of real issues, can do much to overcome student apathy. Attention can be focused on questions of concern to various campus groupings by a party's action in incorporating a proposed solution into its platform. Elections can become more than personality contests by the adoption of slates of candidates by each party. Real understanding can be developed between the aspirant to office and the individual student through active precinct workers.

It should be understood, however, that little good will come from a party system if it is left to languish between campaigns. The danger of the party being controlled by special class, fraternal, or other special interest groups is the major threat to the value of political parties. Too often they are small versions of some of the worst political machines in our city, state, and national political life.

Functions of student governing groups

The student governing group generally performs its duties in one of three ways. It may both develop policy and administer programs. This procedure has the disadvantage of keeping everything centered in a small group. The student government may delegate responsibility for various activities to already existing boards, committees, and organizations and serves as a co-ordinating agency.

The third method used to implement student government is the subcommittee or commission system. A number of subcommittees or commissions work directly under the student governing policy developing group. Where there are large numbers of students this subgroup system is feasible and quite successful. It requires, however, good administrative personnel who can serve in responsible co-ordinating roles. The use of the term commission for these subgroups may imply that they have more status than committees and may be more permanent.

The area within which a student group governs is determined in large measure by how effective it is in terms of its purposes and how these purposes relate to the philosophical concepts of the administration and faculty. The area of operation is determined by a multitude of factors; the experience of students and administration in student self-government; the willingness of students to accept responsibility; the students' knowledge of the needs and skills involved in any given area; the amount of interest in student government shown by administration and faculty.

The successful operation of student governing groups demands a clear understanding between students and administration of the specific limits of student jurisdiction. A verbal understanding is not satisfactory because of the comparatively rapid change of student personnel involved. The jurisdiction that any student government has is a matter to be resolved mutually by the students, faculty, and administration of the institution.

ACADEMIC AFFAIRS—The role of the student government in the academic life of the college needs to be studied and expanded in many institutions. Since the academic education of the student is presumed to be the prime aim of higher education, the student should be vitally concerned with teaching methods, curriculum, and the library. The student government can be an effective means of initiating the participation of students in the academic planning groups of the campus. It can also be the structure for developing programs for faculty advising, new student orientation, faculty evaluation, honor systems, and course planning and evaluation. The role of the student in this area may vary from working at planning and policy levels to actual student services such as advising and tutoring.

DEVELOPING STUDENT MORALE—Developing student morale

on a campus is a positive approach to student discipline. Policies and standards concerning campus behavior should be developed by student and faculty groups. Assemblies, discussions, and other programs dealing with the attitude, social norms, and behavior patterns of the campus can be planned by the student government with faculty assistance to give a constructive approach to the problems of student morale.

The effectiveness with which student government deals with disciplinary questions depends on the respect in which the student governing body is held by the students and the amount of practical authority delegated by the administration. The student government must never curry favor by sensational or created situations, nor must it abuse authority. The extent to which it can manage disciplinary rules will vary with its desire to handle certain difficult situations, the reluctance of the administration to relinquish certain disciplinary controls, and the impracticality of supervision in certain fields. Each of these conditions of the exercise of disciplinary powers by the student government will differ in various schools according to the length of time that student government has existed and how well it has discharged its responsibility. Constructive action in cases of student riots, demonstrations, strikes, and inappropriate personal social behavior can do much to further the cause of student government.

A student governing group, however, should not seek to exercise disciplinary responsibility until it is well established in other spheres of activity as well, for premature action in matters of discipline can do much to weaken or destroy its total effectiveness. The governing body must be careful not to become merely a police force on the campus.

Frequently student discipline responsibilities are handled by a student court which may be a branch or committee of the central student government. If the institution has a law school, law students might well serve on the court. Institutions using the student court to assist with student discipline have found it most effective when it actually has some authority. Students might also serve as members of a campuswide student conduct committee.

CO-ORDINATING ACTIVITIES—The student government fulfills one of its functions when it stimulates and co-ordinates all campus activities. It must go further by providing a well-rounded activity program where one is needed. In this case it may either take upon itself the role of initiator or may delegate this task to committees or organizations. Unless the college is small most of the responsibility for social, recreational, and cultural activities must be assumed by other groups with the student government acting only in an advisory or co-ordinating capacity.

Among its programs are the enhancing of campus social life and the betterment of cultural facilities. It may oversee the physical and economic welfare of the individual student through the investigation of student living and eating conditions, student housing facilities, cost of living, and student wages. It may actually manage student enterprises such as food services and bookstores. It may provide and manage intercollegiate and intramural athletic programs for men and women or work with the councils dealing with these activities. The supervision of college publications including newspapers, magazines, handbooks, and annuals may be the responsibility of some student governments. It certainly should have a strong voice in the general supervising of all student activity finances.

Most student governing groups sponsor many of the college-wide events of the year. Among these activities are student elections, home-coming, parents' week ends, international weeks and seminars, orientation weeks, career conferences, leadership training programs, student government emphasis weeks, pep meetings, talent revues, and campus community chests.

The student government has a special responsibility for supplementing the academic program of the college through the sponsorship of lectures, convocations, or forums on issues of the day. It should attempt to lead the way in the local solution to such national problems as discrimination against minority groups, low student wages, and the shortage of housing facilities.

Other areas in which student governing groups are working are student rights and responsibilities, academic freedom, human relations, national educational issues, and international affairs. There may be permanent committees in these areas, studies might be conducted, and recommendations made for cooperative student and faculty action.

Student government should share the responsibility for evaluation and recognition of new organizations which apply for charters on campus and periodic re-evaluation of campus organizations. Recognition should be based on criteria which are standard and accepted by both students and administration.

Representation of student opinion on faculty-administration committees is a very important function of the student government. Here students through elected or selected representatives are able to express opinions and present points of view which are invaluable to professors and administration. Policies developed with students are more readily held to by the student body than those imposed. Such a medium as student government is highly desirable for this task because it brings out constructive criticism which might, under ordinary circumstances, never be heard. It probably is in this area that the student can make one of his greatest contributions.

Financing student governing groups

Basic to the functioning of good student government are its financial resources. The lack of financial resources has so cur-

tailed the activities of some governing groups that they have
found it necessary to spend more time studying new monetary
sources than in performing their main role. The sources of finances most commonly utilized by a council include (1) grants
from the college or university administration; (2) compulsory
student body fees or taxes; (3) voluntary student body fees;
(4) and earnings from dances, social functions, student stores,
food services, publications, dramatic and musical activities,
and athletics.

The first source means the granting by the administration
of a sum of money to the student government for its purposes.
Though such a system may reflect a realization of the fact
that student activities are an important part of the total college
program, it has the definite disadvantage of dependence upon
the administration for financial stability.

The results of some studies of student governments indicate
that those with compulsory student body fees are generally
the most effective. The compulsory fee guarantees the council
a definite sum each year and distributes the costs equally over
every member of the student body, and if voted on annually
by the student body is definitely democratic.

The voluntary fee necessitates a membership drive each year.
The amount of income from payment of these fees cannot
be determined until the drive is over, and early budgeting is
made difficult.

Raising money by providing specific goods and services is
effective if the student government operates either alone or
cooperatively with the administration and faculty. The types
of services are limited only by the ingenuity of the student
council. Activities such as bookstores, clothing shops, beauty
shops, banking services, barber shops, food services, and gift
shops are among those enterprises managed by student government. Here again, however, receipts can only be estimated,
making planning ahead a matter of speculation.

Perhaps the least effective method for fund raising is that of using special events such as dances, picnics, convocations and concerts as the chief source. Fund raising activities for particular needs such as a scholarship for foreign students is in a different perspective and has its place in the campus milieu.

How to organize for student government

Within the confines of what we know as the democratic system of government are a number of institutionalized forms which blend into the total pattern. Student government is one of these forms and differs little from others in that it requires a commitment for the democratic method on the part of students, the administration, and the faculty. It is impossible to state with any degree of certainty that one manner of organizing student government is better or more effective than another. The situation on each campus is peculiar to that campus and must be dealt with according to the needs, resources, and climate of the institution. The constitution of a student government of a campus of given size and character is not necessarily the constitution for a similar institution. There are, however, several basic steps to be taken in initiating student government in order to insure its success.

Those interested and convinced of the need for student government should become familiar with the literature available on the subject. They should know exactly what the history of it has been on their own campus. They should know the attitude of the administration to student government. Meaningful interviews with students and conferences with student groups are essential.

Student committees or study groups can spend an entire college year or even two exploring the type of student participation in college government that a campus desires. One successful step which has been used is to sponsor a week-end conference or workshop involving the president and the administration, the student organization leaders, the faculty, and alumni. Working papers should be developed by the planning committee and given to the participants ahead. A handbook like this one would be good resource material and additional sources are listed in the bibliography. The conference needs to approach the issue from points of view of the ideal types of student participation in the country today, and the characteristic features of the local campus. It is important that the participants of the conference represent all aspects of the college community. Involvement in the development of the student government is apt to mean more positive and constructive attitudes toward it. A systematic confrontation of all issues is too much to expect, but the general direction for the development of a student government program can be the result of a workshop.

It is important to keep the constitution simple but complete with most of the specific details in the bylaws. If the governing board is the legislative group of the student association, then the constitution is that of the student association with just one section of it describing the function and personnel of the governing board. Details should be included concerning judicial powers and functions, and the duties of the executives need to be stated.

The concept of a community conceived within the institution appears fundamental. The idea of students, faculty, or administration living in different worlds on the same campus does not help the successful organization or operation of student government. The polarity which is so apparent on many campuses today is manifested in friction on matters of common interest and concern to both students and administration. Unless cordial and close relationships and the tranquillity of honest intellectual difference, as opposed to lack of understanding between students and administration, are returned to the campus, higher education may not best serve its function. Student government, if properly guided and intelligently participated in, can be a strong influence for producing better education.

Governing groups in student residences

Whether living units are large or small they provide an opportunity for self-government. Although individual houses may be part of a larger house or residence halls association, they need to develop house organizations with officers, a program of activities, and house policies. The fraternity and sorority houses are more easily organized. College residence hall units usually have special staffs assigned to them to provide counseling for activities. However, for the independent house to maintain a strong organization from year to year requires real effort and interest.

Acceptance and security within one's living unit is important for the college student. To meet these needs a student must have a good social and cultural program, interest in intramural and campus recreation activities, and a desire to maintain good study and living conditions.

If a house maintains a reading room, entertains faculty, parents, and other guests, has speakers and discussions, as well as other educational activities, it can also be a real means of providing a cultural education for its members. The educational and social values that can be accrued through strong living groups are yet to be attained on many campuses.

The student house is usually the basic organization on the campus. In it is the first group of individuals the new student gets to know. Its role in the life of the student is important and needs to receive real consideration when planning and developing student government on a campus.

THE INTER-FRATERNITY AND INTER-SORORITY COUNCIL—Social and fraternal groups are usually members of a council. The most frequent type of inter-house organization is the inter-fraternity or inter-sorority council. These groups consist of representatives from the member houses or groups and usually pay dues according to the size of the house. As is true of any inter-group council, the organization is only as strong as the representatives sent by the member sororities or fraternities. To prevent the development of policies from inadequate representation, many campuses have developed presidents' councils. One college which has had weak council representation now requires that the members be one of the top three ranking officers of each fraternity.

The inter-fraternity or inter-sorority councils differ somewhat from other councils in that they usually formulate and enforce special regulations concerning fraternities and sororities. Pledging, rushing, scholarship, leadership training, buying cooperatives, public relations, intramurals, and social activities are all part of the council program. To help them enforce their regulations they may have judicial committees to which infractions are referred and through which hearings are held.

Although the fraternal movement has been greatly criticized in this country, fraternities can serve sound educational objectives. The inter-fraternity and inter-sorority council can do a great deal to improve the particular fraternal system on a campus. They should be concerned not only with public relations of a cursory nature, but should urge the member organizations to conduct themselves in such a manner and to sponsor types of activities which the community will respect and which will help the individual member to get the most from his or her fraternal experience.

THE RESIDENCE HALLS ASSOCIATION—A large single residence hall is best divided into small units or house groups. The ideal size would be from twenty-five to forty for a house unit. These various units within one hall or in several residence halls can be associated together in a hall council. House representatives to this body may be the house president, one of the house officers, or may be elected at large. Several campuses have inter-hall associations as well as house presidents' councils. In this case the association frequently plans most of the activities and develops the major policies and the house presidents' council serves as a more informal group for the exchange of ideas and programs.

Residence hall associations serve a variety of functions. Frequently they are more meaningful to the individual student in terms of self-government than is the over-all campus governing organization.

In addition to regular standing committees such as the public relations committee, the intra-mural committee, and the social committee, a residence association may have some special activities which will need policy and planning committees. A residence hall store might well be operated by the student residents. The dining rooms may have a student commons committee to confer concerning rates and to relay student opinions concerning the food service. There may have to be a special committee on student conduct or a judicial committee to deal with social conduct. The houses may be concerned with the scholarship of the residents and develop a central committee to secure the averages of the students from the college record office and to plan some inter-house scholastic competition. If the building has a library, the association would want to have a committee to select the books and to develop policies concerning their use.

Lounges and hallways in dormitories usually have a great deal of wall area which makes excellent art exhibit space and would call for an art or exhibits committee. Residence associations might develop speaker's bureaus to help houses secure speakers, develop small instrumental and choral groups, and even publish their own newspapers. Even though a campus has a photography club, a crafts club, and other hobby groups, on large campuses the residence association may well develop its own interest and hobby groups. It is important, however, that students do not become so insular within their living groups that they will not get to know students living in other types of student housing or in other sections of the campus. Independent houses, fraternal groups, and residence halls should plan regularly to do a number of events together enabling them to think of themselves as part of a total college community.

THE INDEPENDENT STUDENT ASSOCIATION—The houses which are not affiliated with the fraternal association or the residence hall association may form an independent student association, or an independent house presidents' council. These may be either as women's and men's organizations or as coed groups. On a number of campuses the residence halls are affiliated with the independent association as well as having an association of their own. The independent student association can sponsor activities similar to those mentioned for dormitories and fraternal groups.

Too frequently the independent is the lost student in the realm of campus life and hence a strong independent student council or association to help integrate the independent into the campus is important in colleges. Because of the constant shifting of residents in independent houses, the houses are difficult to keep organized. Councils and associations for these houses need to conduct leadership training conferences, issue helpful printed notices and newsletters, and provide services which will help the independent houses develop a program to meet the needs of the residents.

Class governing groups

Class organizations have for years been strong groups on the campus. In recent years many have changed in character and have become less steeped in tradition. Class organizations have developed the service concept in place of the traditional hazing and social activities. In place of hazing, orientation programs are conducted. If students select their majors at the end of the sophomore year, the junior class may plan a conference on how to select a major or one dealing with career and vocational information. A senior class on one campus made a study of the placement services available to seniors and designated that their class gift be used to set up a more complete college placement service and office.

In addition to officers, the formation of a council has advantages. It gives more members of the class the opportunity to share in the planning and organizing of class activities and policies. Strong class organizations help develop alumni relations in the years ahead.

Men's and women's student governing groups

Historically women's student governments have been stronger and more influential on the American campus than men's student governments. This is due partially to the fact that frequently women students have had special hours and appear to have certain educational, vocational, and social needs which motivated the development of their own governmental organizations.

Some institutions still have no central student government but have separate government groups. In other institutions, the men's and women's governments are co-ordinated with the student council.

If it is deemed necessary to have separate governing groups for men and women, they should be integrated with the central governing agency. It is also wise to co-ordinate the men's and women's housing governing groups with the men's and women's organizations. Men's and women's government organizations should not exist just because of tradition; they should meet the real needs of the particular campus. They can serve very legitimate purposes, but in no way should duplicate the functions of the main student government group.

The student union

Great conflicts usually arise from a lack of understanding of the functional relationships of the central student governing agency and councils or boards governing unions. If the philosophy of the community is held to on a campus, then the union group should be a body closely co-ordinated and integrated with the student government.

The union building or student center is one of the recreational facilities of the campus. Basically programs and activities should be the responsibility of recognized groups, with the union planning programs only where they have not already been prepared by other basic interest groups. The student government on a campus can provide the perspective to insure that all groups serve their true function in the community.

The financing of the union's program should be part of the central student fee and related to the general activity finance supervision program of the student government.

The whole concept of the college union is in a state of transition. Whether or not there should be one building which serves as a center for social and cultural activities on a campus or several centers is debatable. If the objective is greater integration of activities with the academic program of the campus, then lounges or centers for students might be located in instructional buildings which give greater opportunity for students and faculty to meet informally. The use of the lounges in residence halls only for students in residence sometimes makes for a "town-gown" feeling with the resident and non-resident members of the student community. These lounges

can be to some degree additional significant centers for all
students.

The relationship and role of student centers needs to be a
concern of the main student government agency on the
campus.

The role of the faculty and the administration

The actual role that students play in the administration of an
institution depends upon the educational philosophy of the
faculty, the administration, and the trustees. The degree to
which students are given responsibility varies with the extent
of the belief and interest in which they are held by the faculty.

In evolving increased student participation in the governing of the college, every instance of student-faculty cooperation and mutual working relationships needs to be developed.
Integrating these concepts of increasing student participation,
however, needs to be done gradually. Many of the informal
aspects of the program might be increased before students are
asked to serve in areas of college administration.

Further, the administration should decide just where jurisdiction in the college for student affairs areas shall lie. If students are given responsibilities, they must understand just what
they are and what authority is given to them. The various
counselors and advisers working with students, as well, need
to know what their authority is and must have the support of
the chief administrators in carrying out their work with students.

One campus has attempted to institute a closer administra-
tion-student and faculty-student relationship establishing a
presidents' council composed of the administrators and the
highest student officials on campus. This council, though
possessing no constitution or formal powers, provides through
its periodic meetings a common background for students and

administration to discuss mutual problems. The council has already developed a cooperative atmosphere which has been of constructive influence in campus affairs.

A college that is committed to increasing student participation in its administration can expect its students to accept their new rights with responsibility. Increased freedom does not mean increased license. Students serving with administrative committees need to show the soundest of judgment and the greatest discretion with confidential information.

Education for leadership must be a responsibility shared by all departments, the instructional as well as the personnel programs of an institution. Participation in the administrative aspects of the entire college community needs to be provided.

Colleges in the world should realize that leaders will always exist, good or bad. Society's leadership may be in the hands of a tyrant or a Lincoln. Leaders can be developed, the kind of leaders the world needs. Institutions must be sure that they are exerting every influence and giving every opportunity to their students to enable true democratic leadership to emerge.

III

The college staff person
and student groups

A responsibility

Within the college community the basic responsibility for student government and activities is usually assumed by a professional staff member, as part of the program of the dean of students or the dean of men and women. However, it may be the direct responsibility of a director of student activities, a co-ordinator of activities, a counselor of activities, a social activities director, a union director, or a member of the personnel program staff.

If one concludes that meaningful experiences are educative, the experiences students have in student government and activities should be considered a part of the educational program of an institution. It cannot be assumed that just engaging in group activities automatically results in educational and meaningful experiences. Students need help in attaining the values that can accrue from group activities. This professional assistance is the responsibility administratively of the personnel program and responsibility, as well, of all of the faculty and administration.

The personnel administrator responsible for activities on a campus will most likely function as administrator with student groups and programs and serve as a co-ordinator and possible trainer of faculty members serving in advising roles with groups. Frequently, the chief personnel administrator or activities director is the student government adviser rather than a faculty member and this practice appears to function best. However, it is important to have faculty members concerned with and involved in the student government programs. They can work with commissions and committees in both adviser and member roles and can work with special programs and projects.

The personnel staff person co-ordinates the activities program and develops with students and faculty the policies which govern it. If the individual is a professional person, the behavioral sciences are recognized as a real source of information and insight to help the student to make his activity experiences real opportunities for learning, particularly in the areas of human behavior. The dimensions of concern for group process as well as the final program results can be the significant contribution of the personnel staff person.

The president of the institution usually is not directly concerned with activity programs except as he participates in campus functions and attends them, but his whole philosophy, approach, and basic concepts determine the role that activities will play in the campus life. He is perhaps closer to the student government program than any other activity. If the president sees activities and group experiences as a meaningful part of the student's education he encourages and supports them with the faculty, administrative, and personnel staff. If he feels that extracurricular activities take too much business off the main street of college life, he may expect the college staff just to tolerate activities and do the best they can to keep students in line, and to see that they have adequate social and recreational life. The president with this point of view does not provide staff facilities for achieving the maximum educational value from group experiences. Presidents are also concerned about the public relations aspect of activities and sometimes this is their sole concern. Since activities are frequently covered by the press and involve the public, the president wants the college to look well. This may or may not cause the adviser to be more concerned with performance and production than the educational processes involved in creative planning.

The financial officer of the college whether his title is controller, financial secretary, or treasurer is again a person concerned with the activities of the campus but, particularly in larger institutions, not directly. He wants them "in line financially" and the budget sound and well planned. The financial officer through a service approach on the part of his staff can contribute a great deal in helping students to learn how to do good financial planning, including learning how to make budgets, to keep accounts, to make reports, and to write requisitions. Whether or not the student activities program has a student financial adviser's office or an office dealing with the finances of activities, the financial officer of the institution can do a great deal to make this aspect of student life effective and sound.

Other administrative officers are involved in the student life program as well. The academic dean or vice president for academic affairs may serve as adviser to honorary groups or be closely interested in cultural and professional activities of the college's departments or schools. Most likely he will be concerned with those groups recognizing scholarship and will encourage the promotion and development of these organizations. The more closely the academic dean works with the personnel program, the more he will understand the real values of student participation in activities. The more the academic administrator is involved, the more he will see that a student's education is an integrated whole and not confined to curriculum and instructional activities as one avenue of education, and extracurricular student activities peripheral to them. Personnel workers need to be constantly concerned that the student life and academic program are integrated as effectively as possible.

Other administrators of the college—public relations officers, the chairmen of departments, the buildings and grounds director—all have real influence and sometimes crucial effect on student life. A department chairman who urges that the department have a professional or cultural group related to its curriculum and encourages the faculty to work with the groups makes a real contribution. A buildings and grounds director or supervisor who does not want students in rooms after certain hours or does not like to have the instructional facilities used for nonacademic purposes may be a critical factor in preventing the development of the program. It is essential that all administrators in the institution, no matter what their level of responsibility or assignment, be helped to appreciate the values to the student's education of group life experience.

The organization-faculty adviser

The role of the faculty member serving as an adviser to student organizations is a most vital one, for the adviser is in the position of working more closely and directly with student groups than any other staff person. An informal sampling of thirty-two colleges in all parts of the country, conducted by a doctoral student in student personnel administration at Teachers College, Columbia University, indicates that all colleges included in the sample required a faculty adviser for each organization. No exceptions were noted. The faculty adviser is in a position to offer an informed point of view and impartial perspective which is of great value to the student group. Because his tenure at the college generally extends over a long period of time, he is in a position to provide the necessary continuity of operation needed to supplement the efforts of students who are members of the organization for no more than four years at the most. Many faculty members find advisory responsibilities offer opportunities to know their students on a closer and more informal basis than that provided through classroom contact. Often such relationships facilitate their understanding of the student and their ability to assist him in more effective academic adjustment. The work of the faculty adviser decentralizes the responsibility of the professional personnel officer and contributes a variety of approaches and points of view to the activity program which would not be available if all advisory functions were to be confined to the personnel office.

The selection of faculty advisers for organizations is made by a variety of methods. In some cases it is by administrative appointment determined most frequently on the basis of the individual faculty member's load of classes, committee memberships, etc. On the basis of their special interest in particular fields, the faculty members have sometimes initiated the establishment of particular organizations or have voluntarily accepted adviserships because of their personal involvement in a particular type of activity. Frequently, student groups make direct advances to the individual faculty member of their choice, often without regard to other responsibilities which he may be carrying. Some college administrations require students to submit several names of faculty members in whom they are interested, and the selection from this group is made by administrative appointment.

In the interest of establishing a high level of mutual satisfaction and cooperation, one quite effective method is to have members of the student group suggest names of advisers they would like and to submit this roster to the personnel office where the list may be screened to eliminate faculty members already carrying a heavy work load or serving in other advisory capacities. The final list is then returned to the group for selective vote.

Whatever method is chosen, the most important phase of

the selection process is that of making provision for mutual understanding of the role to be assumed by the faculty adviser. Before consent to serve in this capacity is given, representatives of the student group should sit down with the prospective adviser to discuss their relationship. The student group needs to indicate clearly their expectation of the adviser's responsibility and extent of participation. In turn, the adviser should delineate clearly his perception of the role and the way in which he finds most satisfaction in working with an organizational group. An effective adviser relationship must needs be grounded in common consent and an understanding of the nature of their cooperative work.

Furthermore, in verifying the function of the faculty adviser to student organizations, each institution has a responsibility of defining the fundamental requirements of organizational advisership. Investigation reveals, however, that such statements of responsibility are seldom incorporated in the procedural materials provided on an institutional level for faculty guidance and orientation. Because institution expectations are not implicitly stated, faculty members frequently feel unsure of the limit or extent of their advisory responsibility. Such clarification needs to be made in each school or college. Administrations should not regard dedicated faculty advising as peripheral work. Faculty assistance to student organizations should be recognized as a positive contribution to the educational community, having a decided impact on individuals and the campus climate.

Over and beyond basic institutional responsibilities, the role the adviser assumes is affected by a number of other factors: the nature of the organization with which he is associated, his area of special interest, and his personality and behavior patterns as they affect his way of working with student groups.

By and large, the function of the adviser is usually defined in one or a combination of the roles discussed below.

THE TRAINER-DIRECTOR—This role is generally assumed by the adviser who is responsible for teaching a particular skill or technique of a performance nature. The coach of athletic teams, the drama director who produces the school play, the director of musical groups and the adviser to publications come under this category.

THE ADVISER-CONSULTANT—The adviser, with this type of responsibility, is available when needed but does not become active in the deliberations of the group unless requested to do so by the students. He may not attend meetings regularly. Instead, he is likely to discuss the agenda of a proposed meeting with the executive group before the session and perhaps join them for evaluation afterward. If he is in attendance at meetings, he enters the discussion upon request for counsel or information or clarification, or when his own judgment indicates the need to point out alternatives, pertinent information, pitfalls, etc.

PARTICIPATING MEMBER—To many personally involved advisers the participant member role is a rewarding but most difficult one to play. In this capacity he shares actively in the work of the group. His contributions are accepted or rejected on the basis of their merit and receive no special consideration because of any status factors resulting from his position as a faculty member. He avoids taking the initiative in introducing ideas or action plans, but his suggestions have value to the group because of his additional training and experience just as any other individual member's contributions have special value because of some unique skill which he possesses. To attain this kind of relationship with a student group is not easy. Willingness to work patiently to prove sincerity of intent is paramount. Because this is a relationship rarely entered into with faculty members, the students will be hard to convince that the adviser is not going to take over control in crucial situations or insist upon decisions being made on the basis of his superior judgment. They will test the limits by asking directly or indirectly for faculty leadership. Only by consistently refusing to take advantage of his status position and by constantly demonstrating his respect and confidence in their abilities will he be accepted as a real participant member.

COMBINATIONS OF ALL THREE—Obviously, although the adviser may most frequently play one of the roles indicated above, upon occasion necessarily he will assume a more eclectic response as the situation demands. No rigidly prescribed mode of behavior can be dictated; the good adviser will necessarily "play it by ear," keeping in mind the responsibility of guiding without dictating, of participating without dominating.

Large numbers of faculty members, not specifically delegated to personnel or student activity duties, assume the role of faculty adviser in every institution of higher learning. The influence they exert in these roles is considerable yet few opportunities are available for specific training in this area. The number of graduate courses whose philosophy and content provide significant training for the prospective faculty adviser are few. To the writers' knowledge, few specific courses are offered in any undergraduate college providing education for individuals entering the teaching profession, notwithstanding the fact that advisory responsibilities are likely to be an integral part of their vocational or avocational life. Such courses are definitely needed and should be established by institutions concerned with the development of future teachers.

In lieu of formal training in this area, in-service training of faculty advisers is a new venture now being entered into by many schools and colleges.

On a quite informal level, conferences initiated by the personnel dean in charge of student activities between the prospective group adviser and the student chairman or president help to orient the adviser to the responsibilities of his job and the expectations of the student group as to his role. Such meetings provide opportunity for both parties concerned to raise questions, share points of view, agree on objectives, determine modes of action, and clear channels of communication. On a more formalized basis, on some campuses, work has been done in the establishment and development of annual seminars or workshops for faculty advisers and student organizational heads.

When evaluation of the advisory role is considered, the question arises as to who should evaluate. The obvious answer would seem to be those in position to know or observe, i.e., the students, the professional personnel staff member in a supervisory role, and the advisers themselves. Evaluation of the faculty adviser role, however, is a delicate area. Frequently, the adviser has a vested interest in the organization which he may have been instrumental in forming. Moreover, a long-time relationship perhaps gives him a feeling of personal possession, so that he tends to dominate and take too active a role in decision-making, a function which by rights should be mainly student.

A college student activities committee or other such policy-making group may well assume responsibility for the establishment and acceptance of a well-conceived evaluation instrument. This group may do a great deal to develop a climate responsive to evaluation of advisory roles on a college-wide basis.

A good evaluative survey technique would be the development on a local institutional level of a series of yardsticks or criteria by which the adviser may measure himself. This may be done introspectively or upon an impersonal basis in a group seminar of advisers. The very secure adviser whose relationship with the group is such that he does not threaten them, can sit down and evaluate the role he is assuming with the student group, not for the purpose of viewing himself as a highly successful or inadequate adviser but as a method of working toward a more effective student organization.

Other types of advisers

Other advisory personnel not directly attached to the college staff exert considerable influence on campus organizations. These include alumni of fraternal groups—social, professional, honorary. Alumni also frequently play focal roles in the functioning of athletic teams. In some cases, alumni retain actual membership within the group in an associate or unofficial capacity. They often have considerable say-so in member selection or as financial adviser. They are sought out as consultants on many matters and give general advice freely.

Chaplains, or religious workers maintained on campus by the three major faiths, frequently assume what amounts to faculty advisory responsibility of organizational groups developed within the framework of their particular faith or denomination. Members of the Newman Club, Hillel, Student Christian Association, and numbers of clubs attached to specific denominations of Protestant faiths look to their religious worker for help and guidance, in addition to personal and religious counseling. Because the total assignment of the campus chaplain is to work with students in these areas, they are perhaps more readily available than the faculty adviser of the group.

Traveling representatives of state and national groups having local campus units also function in an advisory capacity and are relied upon by student groups. Personnel from the central office of Greek organizations having national affiliations are regular campus visitors and represent potent factors in the establishment of policy and maintenance of standards by local groups. Where the campus community participates in such national movements as World University Service or the National Student Association, visits by traveling personnel provide opportunities to integrate local efforts with the national scene and to benefit from the thinking and accomplishments of the nationwide organization. On college campuses where the development of teachers is a professional goal, the National Education Association provides excellent consultative service for local affiliates on the student level. Again the various religious faiths send special workers to visit and to co-ordinate the work of groups on many campuses.

The professional personnel staff member has a responsibility to effectively integrate the resources provided by all of these attendant contacts. To maintain good staff liaison with alumni representatives, with the campus chaplain, and with the visiting national consultant is extremely important. These people provide a point of view and perspective which can be utilized most constructively to increase the scope of the total student organizational program.

A few institutions use students who have had special training programs as advisers of student groups. This type of program calls for well organized selection and training experiences in those institutions. Where this is done well, the student adviser is very effective. It does not appear to these writers to be the sole answer to the problem of securing advisers of student groups for it tends to create an even greater schism in the campus faculty-student community.

APPENDIX:

A MODEL CONSTITUTION

Description of the hypothetical university for which the constitution is written:

John Lane University is a school of ninety-five hundred students located in the Middle West. It is a private university with some endowment but with higher than average tuition fees. The university is comprised of a liberal arts college, a college of law, a college of medicine, a college of education, a college of business administration, a college of journalism, a graduate school, a college of engineering, a college of social work. As an institution, it was founded in the late eighteen hundreds and maintains a reputation for excellent academic and professional training. The admissions standards have been high.

The university is located in a city of several hundred thousand people and occupies several blocks in the heart of an urban community. It does have a campus. One-third of the students commute, one-third of the student body is in residence halls, a sixth living in fraternity and sorority houses, and a sixth living in cooperative and other types of student residence situations. It has a very fine student center building which, however, has become too small for the large enrollment. One of the issues of the university is whether to add to the student union or to add other small centers for students to gather in other buildings and locations throughout the campus. The student union has the disadvantage of being located at one end of the campus.

The president of John Lane University has been there for approximately eight years. He came from a liberal arts college with a fine reputation for academic freedom, democratic participation, and high academic standards. He believes that the making of major university decisions and policies must be shared by the university faculty and by students. He realizes, however, that as a president everyone must understand that sometimes his stand may differ from that which comes from policy committees. He is responsible to a rather strong board of trustees all of whom, however, believe in him and his philosophical concepts of working with the faculty and students. Initially they may have been somewhat sceptical of some of his proposals for university reorganization in terms of student participation, but the continued strong contributions of the students have proved to the trustees that they do add a dimension to the policy development program that will make the institution a better institution and give the students an opportunity to learn what constitutes a democracy from firsthand experience.

Administratively, the college consists of a president, a vice president for academic affairs to co-ordinate the colleges administered by individuals with the rank of dean, and a dean of students to co-ordinate the student life program which includes all areas as traditionally thought of in a student personnel program. The dean of students and the vice president of academic affairs are both directly responsible to the president and serve as a close team with him. They hold daily half-hour meetings with him.

The president, the vice president of academic affairs, the dean of students, the deans of the colleges, four elected faculty representatives and two students sit on the Administrative Council of the university. This is the major policy, planning, and development group of the university. The president of the University Student Association and one other student have seats on the council. Students have been serving on the Administrative Council for three years. This was a difficult program for the president to sell to the faculty but they first agreed to have the students sit with the council without vote. Finally, with the reorganization of the university, the students were given two seats with a vote on the council.

Students have been informally invited through the years to contribute their opinion and to serve on special subcommittees of other university committees but not until the coming of the present president did they have seats on the committees. At the same time that the Administrative Council was reorganized, the president urged that all university committees invite some student participation. Hence, during the past three years, the various university committees including curriculum, admissions, etc. studied the role that students might play on their committees. They have invited anywhere from one to five students to be voting members of their committees. Some of the students served for one year, some for two, depending upon the wishes of the particular committee. The Cabinet of the University Student Association appoints the students, but the committees decide which of the students on their committee will sit on the Cabinet of the University Student Association.

All of the student activities and finances are handled by a series of commissions responsible to the student government. These commissions have full responsibilities for recommending the budget for the major activity areas of the campus which use general student funds. Six or seven years ago, these had been faculty and alumni committees. They are now student commissions with some faculty and, in some cases, alumni participation. On all of these commissions, staff members responsible for the activity areas are voting members and have all the rights and responsibilities of the commission. The Finance Commission recommends the budget for the other commissions to the Cabinet of the University Student Association which, in turn, approves it for the coming year. The ultimate power for the budget lies within the hands of the president of the university and the board of trustees. In the whole history of the new student activities budget program they have never had to take action or differ with the student recommendations.

The president says that the heart of the whole program of administration at John Lane University is good communication. The faculty and students are informed of each other's concerns and work as maturely as possible in terms of joint decisions.

The constitution of the John Lane University Student Association which follows describes how this type of student participation and university government functions. Most student governments have a set of Rules and Regulations which deal with more specific details of administration and program.

THE CONSTITUTION OF JOHN LANE UNIVERSITY STUDENT ASSOCIATION

PREAMBLE

[States aims and purposes. Indicates source of responsibility and authority.]

The students, faculty, and administration with the approval of the Board of Trustees of John Lane University hereby establish the John Lane University Student Association. The Association shall be the means whereby students of the University share in the administration and government of the University. The responsibilities herein stated are those which all segments of the University recognize as the privileges, rights, and responsibilities of students.

ARTICLE I. Name

[States name of organization.]

The name of this organization shall be the Student Association of John Lane University.

ARTICLE II. Membership

[Defines membership.]

All students matriculated and registered in John Lane University shall be members of the Student Association. Faculty members and adminstrators elected or appointed to serve on various committees and commissions of the Association shall have the rights and privileges of members of the Association.

ARTICLE III. Officers

[Lists officers, their qualifications, length of office, the method of election and replacement.]

1. The officers of the Association shall be as follows:

A. A *President* who is to be elected from the Junior or

Senior class and who has served on the Cabinet of the Association for at least one semester.

B. A *Vice President* who is to be elected from the Junior or Sophomore class and who has served for at least one semester as a member of the Cabinet of the Association.

C. A *Recording Secretary* who is to be elected from the Sophomore, Junior, or Senior class and who has served at least one semester as a member of the Cabinet of the Association.

D. A *Corresponding Secretary* who is to be elected from the Sophomore, Junior, or Senior class and who has served at least one semester as a member of the Cabinet of the Association.

E. A *Treasurer* who is to be elected from the Junior or Senior class and who has served for at least one semester as a member of the Finance Commission of the Cabinet.

2. The officers shall all serve for a university year.

3. The officers shall be elected to office at annual spring university-wide student elections.

4. The Cabinet of the Association may elect temporary officers to fill vacancies until such time as an all-university election can be held.

ARTICLE IV. Meetings
[Frequency of meetings. Special meetings and who calls them.]

1. There shall be a minimum of one all-university Student Association meeting each semester of the university year.

2. Special meetings may be called by the Cabinet of the Association or by petition of 5 per cent of the members of the Association.

ARTICLE V. Executive Agency
[Describes the function, the membership, and constituent groups of the administrative executive agency of the organization.]

1. The Cabinet shall be the executive and administrative agency of the Association.

2. The function of the Cabinet shall be to carry on the business and program of the Association. It will co-ordinate all the student activities of the University. It will be the clearing center for all student responsibilities in student front committees.

3. The members of the Cabinet shall be:
    a. The elected officers of the Association.
    b. One representative of each class of the University elected at the annual elections.
    c. One representative from each college of the University elected at the annual election.
    d. The chairmen of the activity commissions of the Cabinet.
    e. A student representative from each of the student-faculty committees of the University appointed by each committee.
    f. A faculty adviser who shall be the Dean of Students or his appointed representative.
    g. Two members of the all-university faculty elected by the faculty.
    h. The membership shall serve for one university year.
    i. Replacements to the Cabinet shall be made by the Cabinet until such elections or appointments from other agencies can take place.

4. The officers of the Association shall serve as officers of the Cabinet.

5. The Commissions of the Cabinet shall be:
    a. The Finance Commission
    b. The Athletic Commission
    c. The Publications Commission
    d. The Residence Halls Commission
    e. The Music Activities Commission
    f. The Speech and Dramatic Activities Commission
    g. The College Student Center Commission
    h. The Student Houses Commission

6. The Cabinet shall establish such committees as it deems necessary to carry out the program of the Cabinet and the Association. Among these shall be included:

       a. The Student Service Committee
       b. The National and International Affairs Committee
       c. The Campus Tradition and Events Committee
       d. The Public Relations Committee
       e. The Elections and Personnel Committee
       f. The Judiciary Committee

7. The Cabinet shall meet once a week. Special meetings may be called by the President or any group of three members of the Cabinet.

8. A quorum shall be a two-thirds majority of the members.

ARTICLE VI. Amendment

[Means of amending the Constitution.]

1. Amendments to the Constitution shall be printed in the university newspaper two weeks prior to the time of spring elections at which time they shall be submitted to the Association for approval.

2. A two-thirds majority shall be necessary for the approval of amendments to the Constitution.

ARTICLE VII. Ratification

[How the Constitution is accepted by the organization.]

1. This Constitution shall be ratified at a student election after it has been printed in the university newspaper and discussed at a meeting open to all students.

2. A two-thirds majority in favor of the Constitution shall be necessary to ratify the Articles.

BYLAWS

I. Duties of Officers

1. The President
   A. He shall preside at all meetings of the Cabinet and the Association.
   B. He shall be the official representative of the Association at public functions and on the administrative council of the University.

2. The Vice President
   A. He shall assume the responsibilities of the President when necessary.
   B. He shall co-ordinate the work of the activity committees.

3. The Recording Secretary
   A. He shall be responsible for keeping a record of the minutes of all Association and Cabinet meetings.
   B. He shall act as historian for the Association and be responsible for all of the official records.
4. The Corresponding Secretary
   A. He shall notify Cabinet members of meetings and post notices of Association meetings.
   B. He shall co-ordinate the correspondence of the Association and serve as general office manager for the Cabinet office quarters.
5. The Treasurer
   A. He shall be responsible for the financial administration and records of the Association and Cabinet.
   B. He shall have a seat on the Finance Commission.

II. Functions of the Commissions

1. The Finance Commission
   A. The Commission shall be responsible for all student activity funds to the Cabinet and the Association.
   B. The Cabinet and the Commissions shall submit annual budget requests to the Commission.
   C. The Commission shall submit the proposed annual budget for all activity expenditures to the Cabinet for approval.
   D. The Commission will consist of:
      The Association Treasurer
      A representative from each Commission
      Two students elected at-large at the spring election
      A chairman appointed by the Cabinet
      A secretary elected by the Commission
      A faculty adviser
      The university Business Manager or his representative
      A Treasurer elected by the Commission
2. The Athletic Commission
   A. The Commission will be responsible for all intercollegiate and intramural student athletics in the University.
   B. The Commission membership will consist of:
      The Association Treasurer
      A student and coaching staff representative from each of the major sports
      The directors of intramural athletics for men and for women
      The Athletic Director

The athletic Business Manager

Two students elected at large at the all-university elections

A chairman appointed by the Cabinet upon recommendation of the outgoing Athletic Commission

A Secretary elected by the Commission

A Treasurer elected by the Commission

3. The Publications Commission

    A. The Commission shall be responsible for all student publications in the University.

    B. The Commission membership will consist of:

        A chairman appointed by the Cabinet upon recommendation of the outgoing Commission

        The editor and faculty adviser of each student publication

        A faculty representative from the College of Journalism

        Two students elected at-large in the all-university spring elections

        A Secretary elected by the Commission

        A Treasurer elected by the Commission

4. The Residence Halls Commission

    A. The Commission will be responsible for the student government and activities program in the university residence halls.

    B. The Commission membership shall consist of:

        The Presidents and staff advisers of each of the residence halls

        A chairman appointed by the Cabinet upon recommendation of the outgoing Commission

        The director of residence halls

        Two students elected at-large from the residents of the halls in the all-university elections

        A Secretary elected by the Commission

        A Treasurer elected by the Commission

5. The Music Activities Commission

    A. The Commission shall be responsible for the co-ordination of all music activities.

    B. The Commission shall consist of:

        A chairman appointed by the Cabinet upon recommendation of the outgoing Commission

        A Secretary elected by the Commission

        A Treasurer elected by the Commission

        The student president and adviser or director of each music organization

        Two students elected at-large

6. The Speech and Dramatic Activities Commission
   A. The Commission shall be responsible for the co-ordination of all speech and dramatic activities.
   B. The Commission membership shall consist of:
      A chairman appointed by the Cabinet upon recommendation of the outgoing Commission
      A Secretary elected by the Commission
      A Treasurer elected by the Commission
      The President and adviser or director of each of the organizations
      The chairman of the Department of Speech
      Two students elected at-large
7. The College Student Center Commission
   A. The Commission shall be responsible for the Student Center Building and the activities program in the building.
   B. The Commission membership shall include:
      A Chairman elected by the Student Association
      A Secretary elected by the Student Association
      A Treasurer elected by the Student Association
      A student representative from each College
      Two students elected at-large
      Two faculty members elected by the faculty
      The Center Director
      A representative from the University Alumni Association
      The President of the University Student Association
8. The Student Houses Commission
   A. The Commission shall co-ordinate the student government and program of all independently operated nonuniversity owned student residences.
   B. The Commission membership shall consist of:
      A chairman appointed by the Cabinet upon recommendation of the outgoing Commission
      A Secretary elected by the Commission
      A Treasurer elected by the Commission
      The Director of Student Housing
      One student for each group of 100 or less with no type of housing having more than 3 representatives

III. Finances

1. All members of the University Student Association shall pay an activities fee determined by the Cabinet with the approval of the Association.

2. The fee shall cover the costs of the university activities which are open to all students. Budgets for the use of the monies shall be submitted to the Finance Commission.

3. The Finances of the Association shall be under the control of the Cabinet.

IV. Student-Faculty Committees

1. The Cabinet shall appoint upon recommendation of the Elections and Personnel Committee student representatives to each of the university student-faculty committees. These committees are at present:

> Student Personnel Program
> Admissions
> Curriculum and Academic Policy
> Public Relations
> Commencement
> Public Events and Convocations
> Library
> Development and Planning
> Student Conduct

2. The Committees will designate one of the student representatives to be a member of the Cabinet.

3. The Cabinet Representative shall report to the Cabinet the activities of the Committee and shall communicate to the Committee the point of view of the Cabinet on matters of mutual concern.

V. Elections

[Details would consist of a set of election rules and regulations.]

1. There shall be an annual spring all-university student election.

2. All candidates for Association offices and positions who are elected by the Association or any segment thereof shall be elected at the time of the spring elections.

VI. Amendments

1. Amendments to the bylaws shall be printed in the university newspaper two weeks prior to the time of being voted on at a Cabinet meeting. Any member of the Association should have the opportunity of stating his opinion at the Cabinet meeting before the amendment is voted on.

2. A three-fourths majority should be necessary for the approval of the amendment.

VII. Ratification

1. These bylaws shall be ratified at a student election after they have been printed in the university newspaper and discussed at a meeting open to all students.
2. A two-thirds majority in favor of the bylaws shall be necessary to ratify the bylaws.

BIBLIOGRAPHY

1. BOOKS, PAMPHLETS, AND MAGAZINES

Beckhard, R., *How To Plan and Conduct Workshops and Conferences.* New York, Association Press, 1956.

Beene, K. D., and P. Sheats, "Functional Roles of Group Members," *Journal of Social Issues.* 4:42-47, 1948.

Cantor, Nathaniel, *Dynamics of Learning*, Buffalo, Foster and Stewart, 1956.

Chase, S., *Roads to Agreement*, New York, Harper & Brothers, 1951.

Conference Leadership. By and Available from Esso Training Center, 1104 Elizabeth Ave., Elizabeth, New Jersey. Free—A test and reference to assist in the development of conference leaders for training programs.

Conference Sense. By the Bureau of Naval Personnel, U. S. Navy. Available from the Superintendent of Documents, Government Printing Office, Washington 25, D. C.

De Huszar, George B., *Practical Applications of Democracy*, New York, Harper & Brothers, 1945.

Educational Film Guide, Krahn, F. A. (Ed.), New York, H. W. Wilson Co., 1953. Annual supplements.

Falvey, Frances E., *Student Participation in College Administration*, New York, Bureau of Publications, Teachers College, Columbia University, 1952.

Frank, Lawrence K., *How To Be a Modern Leader*, New York, Association Press, 1954.

Gordon, Thomas, *Group-Centered Leadership*, Boston, Houghton, Mifflin Co., 1955.

Gouldner, Alvin W., (Ed.), *Studies in Leadership: Leadership and Democratic Action*, New York, Harper & Brothers, 1950.

Haiman, Franklyn S., *Group Leadership and Democratic Action*, Boston, Houghton Mifflin Co., 1950.

Hall, D. M., *The Dynamics of Group Discussion*, Danville, Ill., The Interstate, 1950.

Hoffmann, Randall W. and Plutchik, Robert, *Small-Group Discussion in Orientation and Teaching*, New York, G. P. Putnam's Sons, 1959.

Homans, George Casper, *The Human Group*, New York, Harcourt, Brace & Co., 1950.

Kelley, Janet A., *College Life and the Mores*, New York, Bureau of Publications, Teachers College, Columbia University, 1947.

Klein, Alan F., *Role Playing in Leadership Training and Group Problem Solving*, New York, Association Press, 1956.

Klopf, Gordon, "Guidance Emphasis in Student Activities," *Guidance in Teacher Education*, 36th Yearbook, 1957. Cedar Falls, Iowa: The Association for Student Teaching.

Klopf, Gordon, *Planning Student Activities in the High School*, Madison, University of Wisconsin Extension Division Press, 1949.

Knowles, M., and Knowles, H., *How To Develop Better Leaders*, New York, Association Press, 1955.

Lloyd-Jones, Esther, and Smith, Margaret Ruth (Eds.), *Student Personnel Work as Deeper Teaching*, New York, Harper & Brothers, 1954.

Lunn, Harry H., Jr., *The Student's Role in College Policy-Making*, Washington, American Council on Education, 1957.

Miles, M. B., *Learning to Work in Groups*, New York, Bureau of Publications, Teachers College, Columbia University, 1959.

Strang, Ruth, *Group Work in Education*, New York, Harper & Brothers, 1958.

Tead, Ordway, *The Art of Leadership*, New York, McGraw-Hill Book Co., 1935.

Tead, Ordway, *The Climate of Learning*, New York, Harper & Brothers, 1958.

Thelen, Herbert A., *Dynamics of Groups at Work*, Chicago, University of Chicago Press, 1954.

Trecker, Audrey and Harleigh, *How to Work with Groups*, New York, Woman's Press, 1952.

Woolf, Maurice D., and Woolf, Jeanne A., *The Student Personnel Program: Its Development and Integration in the High School and College*, New York, McGraw-Hill Book Co., 1953.

Wrenn, C. Gilbert, *Student Personnel Work in College, with Emphasis on Counseling and Group Experience.* New York, The Ronald Press Company, 1951.

2. FILMS

How to Conduct a Discussion, Wilmette, Ill., Encyclopaedia Britannica Films.

Let's Discuss It, New York, National Film Board of Canada.

Meeting in Session, New York, Bureau of Publications, Teachers College, Columbia University.

Our Invisible Committees, Washington, National Training Laboratories.

Room for Discussion, Wilmette, Ill., Encyclopaedia Britannica Films.

3. UNITED STATES NATIONAL STUDENT ASSOCIATION PUBLICATIONS

Student Government

Brock, Elmer Paul, *A Call to Order* (Guide to Parliamentary Procedure). Philadelphia, USNSA, 1954. Simplified handbook on parliamentary procedure for student governments and campus organizations, designed to introduce the student to the accepted rules of order and to provide a handy reference and supplement to Robert's Rules.

Filerman, Gary. *Human Relations Problems and Programs: A Casebook.* Minneapolis, USNSA, 1959. A compilation of cases representing problems in campus human relations and illustrating ways in which these problems can be approached. Prepared for the First National Intercollegiate Human Relations Workshop.

Glass, Stanford, *Guides for the Student Body President,* Philadelphia, USNSA, 1956. A functional and philosophical analysis of the nature and duties of the chief office in campus government.

Green, Reginald H., *The College Student and the Changing South,* Philadelphia, USNSA, 1959. A consideration of the problems of race relations confronting the southern campus and its student body.

Green, Reginald H., and Coleman, Elnora H., *The Student's Stake in Academic and Educational Freedom,* Philadelphia, USNSA, 1959.

Preston, Gene, *Campus Justice,* Philadelphia, USNSA, 1956. Study of the history, purposes and operation of student self-discipline, emphasizing student participation in campus judicial systems.

Staff, *The Tools of Giving*, Philadelphia, USNSA, 1954. Descriptions of various campus fund-raising drives, suggested guides in making allocations, and administrative techniques and practices.

Werner, Fred, *Casebook of Student Government Materials*, Philadelphia, USNSA, 1959.

Werner, Fred, *Freshman Orientation: A New Meaning*, Philadelphia, USNSA, 1958. An evaluation of orientation programs with suggestions for a new approach; emphasizes the role of the student and faculty; outline for a year-round program.

Werner, Fred, *Honor Systems in Higher Education*. (Revised) Philadelphia, USNSA, 1959. Discussion of the objectives and essentials of an honor system; provides information for establishing an honor system.

Wilcox, G., and Brock, Elmer, *Functioning Leadership Training Programs*, Philadelphia, USNSA, 1953. Specific programming for leadership training as well as techniques, organization, and use of the group method.

Student Affairs

Casey, Florence, *Public Relations Primer*, Philadelphia, USNSA, 1959. A discussion of public relations programs for student leaders.

Green, Reginald, *College Unions: Laboratories for Learning*, Philadelphia, USNSA, 1958. A study of goals, programs, structures, administration, finance. Detailed bibliography. Includes articles by union and student personnel administrators. Produced in cooperation with the Association of College Unions.

Green, Reginald, *Student Fitness: Campus Programming for Health and Safety*, Philadelphia, USNSA, 1958. An over-all approach illustrated by examples and case studies of student participation in health services, health education, and healthful environment.

Kahn, Ed., and Green, Reginald, *Mass Communication on Campus*, Philadelphia, USNSA, 1958. A study of communication theory and practice, rights and responsibilities, opportunities and obligations as they relate to the campus press. Case studies, discussion questions, and extensive sample articles.

Harrington, James, *A Student Discount Service Program for You*. Philadelphia, USNSA, 1959. A discussion of the operation of an SDS program with tips on the organization and establishment of an effective program for your campus.

International Affairs

Jones, Peter, *USNSA and IUS Relations,* Cambridge, USNSA, 1956. Detailed study of the relations between USNSA and the Communist-dominated International Union of Students, 1946-1956.

Lunn, Harry C., *How To Run a Campus International Program,* Cambridge, USNSA, 1954. The role of the international campus administrator and the organization of student government international and travel programs.

Lunn, Harry C., *Student Government and Foreign Student Programming,* Cambridge, USNSA, 1954. Complete background and organization of student government programs for foreign students. Specific project suggestions included.

Staff, USNSA International Affairs Brochure. Cambridge, USNSA, 1958. Descriptive folder suitable for mass distribution, explains purposes, policies, and programs of USNSA's International Affairs Commission.

Student Responsibility

Green, Reginald, *Responsibility in Student Affairs, Commission Study Series, No. 3,* Philadelphia, USNSA, 1958. Student personnel services, living groups, athletics, economic welfare, health, student housing, social and cultural programs, values, student unions.

Green, Reginald and Coleman, Elnora, *Entering the Academic Vocation: What Can the Student Do?,* Philadelphia, USNSA, 1959. A description of student and student government participation in encouraging increased consideration of college teaching as a vocation. Views campus attitudes, informational programs, undergraduate participation in instructional activity.

Green, Reginald and Coleman, Elnora, *Student Responsibility In Counseling, Tutoring, Advising,* Philadelphia, USNSA, 1959. An examination of the rational needs and opportunities for student counseling and counseling assistance. Academic, tutorial, dormitory, fraternity, and counseling center cases cited.

Green, Reginald and Coleman, Elnora, *Student Contributions to Institutional Self Study,* Philadelphia, USNSA, 1959. An evaluation and exploration of the bases and needs for student and student organizational contributions to all-campus evaluations and critiques. Discussion of achieved and potential work in curricular activity, facility, instructional, and development plan study.

Green, Reginald H., *Better Higher Education for More Students,* Philadelphia, USNSA, 1959. (Backgrounds and Bases of Student Responsibility.) An over-all programing guide based on the Ford Foundation financed Student Responsibility Project. Includes a critical examination of the concept and applications of student responsibility: details actual student work to improve campus attitudes toward the academic, increases institutional resource utilization, participates in instructional programing development and operation, encourages consideration of the academic vocation, and participation in the development of improved counseling services.

Green, Reginald H., *Student Responsibility: A Final Report to the Ford Foundation,* Philadelphia, USNSA, 1959. A survey and evaluation of the goals, programs, and results of the Student Responsibility Project on the national, regional, and campus levels.

Staff, *The Idea of a Student,* Philadelphia, USNSA, 1958-59. A serious evaluation of the aims and opportunities of the student and his resultant obligations and rights. Examination of the need for students to be educated through active rather than passive participation. Deals both with the campus framework and the broader issues and ideas which are of concern to the student.

Johnson, Willard and Coleman, Elnora, *Student Responsibility in Higher Education,* Philadelphia, USNSA, 1958. A guide to campus programing in teacher recruitment, student counseling, and guidance, and improving student attitudes toward learning.

Kiley, Robert R., *Responsibility in Student Government, Commission Study Series, No. 1,* Philadelphia, USNSA, 1958. Structure, administration, relations with other organizations, student self-discipline, leadership training.

Larkin, Bruce, *Student Responsibility in International Affairs, Commission Study Series, No. 4,* Cambridge, USNSA, 1958. International student organizations, student exchange, foreign student programing, relations with student groups overseas.

Lunn, Harry, *The Student's Role in College Policy-Making,* Washington, 1957, American Council on Education. Historical and philosophical study, discussion of problem areas in developing student participation in institutional policy-making and administration.

USNSA Organization

Preston, Gene, *USNSA in the Region.* (A Manual of Administration and Organization.) Philadelphia, USNSA, 1956, (Revised, 1958)

Regional programing and responsibilities, with extensive how-to information for regional officers.

Staff, *USNSA on Campus.* (Revised 1959) Philadelphia, USNSA. Handbook for student body presidents, NSA campus co-ordinators, and other student officers responsible for activating the services and interpreting the purposes of USNSA on the individual campus.

Staff, *USNSA Descriptive Brochure.* Philadelphia, USNSA, (Revised 1958). (Descriptive folder suitable for mass distribution, explains organization, purposes and policies of USNSA.)

Staff, *Summary Report, USNSA,* Philadelphia (current year). Review of twelve months' activities, including major actions of the National Student Congress. Program for current year. Available after October 1.

Staff, *Codification.* Philadelphia, USNSA (current year). A compilation of all existing policies of the United States National Student Association through legislation passed by the elected representatives of American students.

Staff, *The National Student News.* Philadelphia, USNSA. Only national newspaper for students. Monthly summary of national and international news concerning students. Eight issues per academic year. Special supplements providing detailed coverage of special areas. Available on individual subscription basis, per year.

Travel Program

Educational Travel, Inc., *Work, Study, Travel Abroad.* New York. Travel Department. Illustrated comprehensive guide to student travel opportunities abroad, contains sections on individual travel, tours, summer sessions, seminars, American colleges abroad, work camps. Revised annually. Available in bulk lots to member school student governments at reduced rates.

INDEX